Endowed by Our Creator

In CONGRESS, July 4, 1776.

The unanimous Declaration of the thirteen united States of America,

When in the Course of human events, it becomes necessary for one people to dissolve the political bands which have connected them with another, and to assume among the powers of the earth, the separate and equal station to which the Laws of Nature and of Nature's God entitle them, a decent respect to the opinions of mankind requires that they should declare the causes which impel them to the separation. —— We hold these truths to be self-evident, that all men are created equal, that they are endowed by their Creator with certain unalienable Rights, that among these are Life, Liberty and the pursuit of Happiness. — That to secure these rights, Governments are instituted among Men, deriving their just powers from the consent of the governed, — That whenever any Form of Government becomes destructive of these ends, it is the Right of the People to alter or to abolish it, and to institute new Government, laying its foundation on such principles and organizing its powers in such form, as to them shall seem most likely to effect their Safety and Happiness. Prudence, indeed, will dictate that Governments long established should not be changed for light and transient causes; and accordingly all experience hath shewn, that mankind are more disposed to suffer, while evils are sufferable, than to right themselves by abolishing the forms to which they are accustomed. But when a long train of abuses and usurpations, pursuing invariably the same Object evinces a design to reduce them under absolute Despotism, it is their right, it is their duty, to throw off such Government, and to provide new Guards for their future security. — Such has been the patient sufferance of these Colonies; and such is now the necessity which constrains them to alter their former Systems of Government. The history of the present King of Great Britain is a history of repeated injuries and usurpations, all having in direct object the establishment of an absolute Tyranny over these States. To prove this, let Facts be submitted to a candid world. —— He has refused his Assent to Laws, the most wholesome and necessary for the public good. —— He has forbidden his Governors to pass Laws of immediate and pressing importance, unless suspended in their operation till his Assent should be obtained; and when so suspended, he has utterly neglected to attend to them. —— He has refused to pass other Laws for the accommodation of large districts of people, unless those people would relinquish the right of Representation in the Legislature, a right inestimable to them and formidable to tyrants only. —— He has called together legislative bodies at places unusual, uncomfortable, and distant from the depository of their Public Records, for the sole purpose of fatiguing them into compliance with his measures. —— He has dissolved Representative Houses repeatedly, for opposing with manly firmness his invasions on the rights of the people. —— He has refused for a long time, after such dissolutions, to cause others to be elected; whereby the Legislative powers, incapable of Annihilation, have returned to the People at large for their exercise; the State remaining in the mean time exposed to all the dangers of invasion from without, and convulsions within. —— He has endeavoured to prevent the population of these States; for that purpose obstructing the Laws for Naturalization of Foreigners; refusing to pass others to encourage their migrations hither, and raising the conditions of new Appropriations of Lands. —— He has obstructed the Administration of Justice, by refusing his Assent to Laws for establishing Judiciary powers. —— He has made Judges dependent on his Will alone, for the tenure of their offices, and the amount and payment of their salaries. —— He has erected a multitude of New Offices, and sent hither swarms of Officers to harrass our people, and eat out their substance. —— He has kept among us, in times of peace, Standing Armies without the Consent of our legislatures. —— He has affected to render the Military independent of and superior to the Civil power. —— He has combined with others to subject us to a jurisdiction foreign to our constitution, and unacknowledged by our laws; giving his Assent to their Acts of pretended Legislation: — For Quartering large bodies of armed troops among us: — For protecting them, by a mock Trial, from punishment for any Murders which they should commit on the Inhabitants of these States: — For cutting off our Trade with all parts of the world: — For imposing Taxes on us without our Consent: — For depriving us in many cases, of the benefits of Trial by Jury: — For transporting us beyond Seas to be tried for pretended offences: — For abolishing the free System of English Laws in a neighbouring Province, establishing therein an Arbitrary government, and enlarging its Boundaries so as to render it at once an example and fit instrument for introducing the same absolute rule into these Colonies: — For taking away our Charters, abolishing our most valuable Laws, and altering fundamentally the Forms of our Governments: — For suspending our own Legislatures, and declaring themselves invested with power to legislate for us in all cases whatsoever. —— He has abdicated Government here, by declaring us out of his Protection and waging War against us. —— He has plundered our seas, ravaged our Coasts, burnt our towns, and destroyed the lives of our people. —— He is at this time transporting large Armies of foreign Mercenaries to compleat the works of death, desolation and tyranny, already begun with circumstances of Cruelty & perfidy scarcely paralleled in the most barbarous ages, and totally unworthy the Head of a civilized nation. —— He has constrained our fellow Citizens taken Captive on the high Seas to bear Arms against their Country, to become the executioners of their friends and Brethren, or to fall themselves by their Hands. —— He has excited domestic insurrections amongst us, and has endeavoured to bring on the inhabitants of our frontiers, the merciless Indian Savages, whose known rule of warfare, is an undistinguished destruction of all ages, sexes and conditions. In every stage of these Oppressions We have Petitioned for Redress in the most humble terms: Our repeated Petitions have been answered only by repeated injury. A Prince, whose character is thus marked by every act which may define a Tyrant, is unfit to be the ruler of a free people. Nor have We been wanting in attentions to our Brittish brethren. We have warned them from time to time of attempts by their legislature to extend an unwarrantable jurisdiction over us. We have reminded them of the circumstances of our emigration and settlement here. We have appealed to their native justice and magnanimity, and we have conjured them by the ties of our common kindred to disavow these usurpations, which, would inevitably interrupt our connections and correspondence. They too have been deaf to the voice of justice and of consanguinity. We must, therefore, acquiesce in the necessity, which denounces our Separation, and hold them, as we hold the rest of mankind, Enemies in War, in Peace Friends. ——

We, therefore, the Representatives of the united States of America, in General Congress, Assembled, appealing to the Supreme Judge of the world for the rectitude of our intentions, do, in the Name, and by Authority of the good People of these Colonies, solemnly publish and declare, That these United Colonies are, and of Right ought to be Free and Independent States; that they are Absolved from all Allegiance to the British Crown, and that all political connection between them and the State of Great Britain, is and ought to be totally dissolved; and that as Free and Independent States, they have full Power to levy War, conclude Peace, contract Alliances, establish Commerce, and to do all other Acts and Things which Independent States may of right do. —— And for the support of this Declaration, with a firm reliance on the protection of divine Providence, we mutually pledge to each other our Lives, our Fortunes and our sacred Honor.

Button Gwinnett
Lyman Hall
Geo Walton.

Wm Hooper
Joseph Hewes,
John Penn

Edward Rutledge 1.

Thos Heyward Junr.
Thomas Lynch Junr.
Arthur Middleton

John Hancock

Samuel Chase
Wm Paca
Thos Stone
Charles Carroll of Carrollton

George Wythe
Richard Henry Lee
Th Jefferson
Benja Harrison
Thos Nelson jr.
Francis Lightfoot Lee
Carter Braxton

Robt Morris
Benjamin Rush
Benja. Franklin
John Morton
Geo Clymer
Jas. Smith
Geo. Taylor
James Wilson
Geo. Ross
Caesar Rodney
Geo Read
Tho M:Kean

Wm Floyd
Phil. Livingston
Frans. Lewis
Lewis Morris

Richd Stockton
Jno Witherspoon
Fras. Hopkinson
John Hart
Abra Clark

Josiah Bartlett
Wm Whipple
Saml Adams
John Adams
Robt Treat Paine
Elbridge Gerry
Step. Hopkins
William Ellery
Roger Sherman
Saml Huntington
Wm Williams
Oliver Wolcott
Matthew Thornton

Endowed by Our Creator

The Bible, Science, and the Battle for America's Soul

John G. West

Seattle Discovery Institute Press 2026

Description

The Declaration of Independence proclaims that "all men are created equal" and "are endowed by their Creator with certain unalienable rights." For generations, those hallowed words inspired not only Americans, but millions around the globe. Yet today many Americans are skeptical or confused about the Declaration's key claims. In this timely book, political scientist John G. West explores the original meaning of the Declaration and shows how its propositions drew support from both the Bible and early modern science. He then documents how science was later misused to overturn the Declaration's teaching on equality, subvert its understanding of liberty, and justify the creation of a technocratic state that regulates us from cradle to grave. Finally, he reveals new scientific discoveries that are pointing us back to the truths expressed in the Declaration—and he explains why it is urgent that our culture recover them.

Copyright Notice

Library Cataloging Data

Endowed by Our Creator: The Bible, Science, and the Battle for America's Soul

by John G. West

Cover design by Nathan Jacobson.

212 pages, 6 x 9 inches

Library of Congress Control Number: 2026932581

ISBN: 978-1-63712-087-3 (paperback), 978-1-63712-089-7 (Kindle), 978-1-63712-088-0 (EPUB)

BISAC: POL072000 POLITICAL SCIENCE / Religion, Politics & State

BISAC: POL030000 POLITICAL SCIENCE / American Government / National

BISAC: HIS036000 HISTORY / United States / General

BISAC: HIS036030 HISTORY / United States / Revolutionary Period (1775–1800)

Publisher Information

Discovery Institute Press, 506 2nd Avenue, Suite 1700, Seattle, WA 98104

Internet: discovery.press

Published in the United States of America on acid-free paper.

First Edition, March 2026

Advance Praise

John West has performed an important role for our 250th birthday as a country. He reminds us that the Founding Fathers meant that our rights come from our Creator. They understood the radicalism of rights coming from God and not secular authority. Our current crisis of culture and spirit will only be healed by the return to those Creator-endowed rights.
—**Newt Gingrich**, Speaker, US House of Representatives (1995–1999)

The Declaration of Independence has been obscured by two-and-a-half centuries of lies, confusion, and cultural decay. John West masterfully peels back the layers of debris to reveal the truth and beauty of America's founding document to a new generation that desperately needs it. An essential primer on the greatest political document in human history—and the Darwinist worldview that tried to kill it.
—**Joel Berry**, Managing Editor, *The Babylon Bee*; co-author of *The Postmodern Pilgrim's Progress*

What could be more important on our celebration of 250 years as a nation than to understand the basis of our divinely blessed founding? This book gets us back to bedrock.
—**Sam Brownback**, former United States Senator and Governor of Kansas and former US Ambassador-at-Large for International Religious Freedom

John West has written an important and wide-ranging book, examining America's founding ideals and the gradual but consistent assault on them through the years. He urges a rededication to the principles enunciated in the Declaration of Independence and underscores our responsibility to pass down these ideas to future generations. His thoughtful work forces us to examine our founding principles from a variety of perspectives and issues, including religion, race, human rights, science, and governance. It couldn't be timelier as we approach America's 250th anniversary celebration.

—**David Limbaugh**, *New York Times* bestselling author of *Jesus on Trial*, *Crimes Against Liberty*, and other books

If you have waited for a book that offers a moral foundation combined with political responsibility compatible with modern science, wait no longer. John West has done it. This masterful work begins with the Declaration of Independence and traces the fundamental truths therein through the complete development of modern scientific culture, along the way settling Darwin in his proper niche and reviving the 'consent of the governed' as the bedrock of good government.

—**William B. Allen**, Emeritus Dean and Professor of Political Philosophy, Michigan State University; former Chairman, United States Commission on Civil Rights

In *Endowed by Our Creator*, John West grasps and wields the redemptive key to prosperity: human creativity in the image of the Creator.

—**George Gilder**, author of *Life After Capitalism* and *Wealth and Poverty*

It is a strong claim to say that America was born in 1776. Why not 1620 with the Mayflower Compact, 1783 with the Treaty of Paris, or 1788 with the ratification of the Constitution? As John G. West eloquently explains, America is founded on a set of ideas, ideas articulated in the Declaration of Independence. Our nation's commitment to these ideas has served us well, but this commitment has been undermined by problematic "scientific" claims (as opposed to true advances in the natural sciences). Dr. West helps us understand how and why this has happened, and he calls upon his fellow citizens to recommit ourselves to the Declaration's principles.

—**Mark David Hall**, Professor, Regent University; author of *Did America Have a Christian Founding?*

Endowed by Our Creator is required reading for every adult citizen and resident of America. It is required reading for every student in our public, private, and home schools as well as colleges and universities. Dr. John West has done the Herculean task of elucidating the meaning and eternal importance of the foundational creed of the United States of America—the Declaration of Independence. And in doing so, West has elegantly and convincingly shown that America's life or death is contingent on our embodiment or rejection of what Abraham Lincoln called "that immortal emblem of Humanity—the Declaration of American Independence." *Endowed by Our Creator* is a call to remember the exceptional founding of our nation and take action to preserve it for the blessing of future Americans and the world.

—**Gerson Moreno-Riaño**, President, Cornerstone University and Cornerstone Theological Seminary

In *Endowed by Our Creator*, John West masterfully exposes how science, philosophy, theology, and political theory have been misused to portray the Declaration of Independence as antiquated and misleading. He demonstrates instead that these disciplines, rightly understood, strongly reinforce the Declaration's original meaning and enduring intent. West's argument decisively restores the Declaration to its proper place: a document—indeed, a creed—whose ideals outlast the flaws of its framers and that remains as sound, inspiring, and aspirational today as it was in 1776.

—**William A. Dembski**, author of *The Design Inference*

John West supplies a succinct analysis of the fundamental principles of the Declaration of Independence. He also shows how contemporary science may supplement and even fulfill those principles against clashing claims from social and natural scientists. Even skeptics may find inspiring the approach he recommends for understanding the 250-year-old document that even now at our best moments guides our national life.

—**Ken Masugi**, Lecturer in Government, Advanced Academic Programs, Johns Hopkins University (2009–2025); co-editor of *The American Founding: Essays on the Formation of the Constitution*

I am too theologically modest to declare how much of the Declaration of Independence should be attributed to divine Providence, but John West is right to direct our attention to the way in which our rights, duties, and free government itself were "endowed by our Creator," and must draw their understanding from "the laws of Nature and of Nature's God." Further, he notes that the Declaration was the object of "veneration" in the deepest sense from the moment it appeared in 1776, which then gets us to the main point—why it still deserves our veneration today, on its 250th anniversary.

—**Steven F. Hayward**, Visiting Professor, Pepperdine University School of Public Policy; author of *The Age of Reagan: The Fall of the Old Liberal Order* and *The Age of Reagan: The Conservative Counterrevolution*

To Harry V. Jaffa (1918–2015)
and Bruce K. Chapman, to whom I owe much.
The light of the Declaration still burns because of such men.

Contents

Figure 1.1. The Declaration of Independence on display in 1943 at the base of the Jefferson Memorial.

1. America's Creed

"America is the only nation in the world that is founded on a creed," observed English writer G. K. Chesterton after visiting the United States in 1921.[1] "That creed is set forth with dogmatic and even theological lucidity in the Declaration of Independence; perhaps the only piece of practical politics that is also theoretical politics and also great literature."

Many Americans are apt to miss the full significance of Chesterton's observation. Throughout human history, nations have defined themselves primarily by ethnicity, geography, or religion. Although Americans do have some of those traditional ties, America has defined herself since July 4, 1776, largely by a commitment to a common set of ideas expressed by the Declaration of Independence.

The Declaration encapsulates those ideas in fifty-five words that have become some of the most famous in the English language: "We hold these truths to be self-evident, that all men are created equal, that they are endowed by their Creator with certain unalienable Rights, that among these are Life, Liberty and the pursuit of Happiness. —That to secure these rights, Governments are instituted among Men, deriving their just powers from the consent of the governed."[2]

Charles Carroll was the lone Catholic to sign the Declaration, and he was its last surviving signer. Reflecting on the document's importance on its fiftieth anniversary in 1826, he recommended "to the present and future generations the principles of that important document, as the best earthly inheritance their ancestors could bequeath to them; and pray[ed] that the civil and religious liberties they have secured to my country may be perpetuated to remotest posterity, and extended to the whole family of man."[3]

Carroll held a glimpse of the future. From the founding of America onward, the Declaration's propositions provided a justification for human rights, limited government, and equal treatment under the law to countless people around the globe. Those propositions also established a standard by which future Americans could judge the actions of themselves and their nation. As Abraham Lincoln pointed out, America's Founders "did not mean to assert the obvious untruth, that all were then actually enjoying [the]... equality" proclaimed by the Declaration; instead:

> They meant simply to declare the *right*, so that the *enforcement* of it might follow as fast as circumstances should permit. They meant to set up a standard maxim for free society, which should be familiar to all, and revered by all; constantly looked to, constantly labored for, and even though never perfectly attained, constantly approximated, and thereby constantly spreading and deepening its influence, and augmenting the happiness and value of life to all people of all colors everywhere.[4]

The Declaration's words indeed became "a standard maxim" that has been revered by Americans from all classes and walks of life. They inspired Lincoln and many others who fought for the abolition of slavery.[5] They were invoked by civil rights protestors in the 1950s and '60s in their efforts to secure equal rights for all.[6]

Over the years, the Declaration has assumed a sacred status in America's civic life. In other countries, people showed their patriotism by making pilgrimages to see the tombs of their leaders. In the Soviet Union and communist China, people went to pay their respects to the embalmed bodies of Lenin and Mao.[7] In America, millions of citizens made a pilgrimage to view a piece of parchment.[8]

Starting in the 1840s, the Declaration was put on nearly permanent public display, usually in the nation's capital.[9] In 1876, the Declaration returned temporarily to Independence Hall in Philadelphia during that city's celebration of the nation's centennial. On

July 4, 1876, tens of thousands flocked to Independence Square next to Independence Hall for a mass celebration featuring a 250-person orchestra and a choir of over a thousand voices.[10] Dignitaries in attendance included the vice president of the United States, the emperor of Brazil, and Civil War general William T. Sherman, now the Commanding General of the United States Army.

The highlight of the celebration was the display and public reading of the Declaration of Independence. The mayor of Philadelphia brought out the original Declaration and showed it to the crowd. According to a report the next day in *The Philadelphia Inquirer*, "As the vast multitude gazed upon the hallowed words, ten thousand throats joined in a shout of acclaim which made the welkin ring. Again and again the huzzas were repeated, each cheer being given with more and more enthusiasm."[11] The governor of Pennsylvania encouraged even more cheering, and "the tens of thousands in the Square united with the thousands on both platforms, and gave the venerated document a shout of welcome of such heartiness and power" that it was heard far along the street on the other side of Independence Hall.

According to the *Inquirer*, "the Mayor several times attempted to withdraw the document proper from public gaze, but it was not until he had held it above the platform for almost ten minutes that he was permitted to lay it upon the table in front." Then Richard Henry Lee of Virginia, a grandson of the signer of the Declaration of Independence of the same name, came forward and read from the original Declaration to more cheers and applause. After the reading, Susan B. Anthony and a group of suffragettes tried to upstage the festivities by delivering a copy of their own "Declaration of Rights of the Women of the United States" to US Senator Thomas Ferry in front of the crowd. He accepted it without a word.[12]

The veneration of the Declaration did not cease after the nation's centennial. By the 1920s and '30s, millions of Americans were traveling to Washington, DC, to view the Declaration at the Library of Congress.[13] During World War II, the Declaration was considered too priceless to remain in the nation's capital and was moved along with other historic documents to Fort Knox in Kentucky to be kept safe.[14] In 1943, the Declaration was temporarily released to be displayed under guard at the dedication of the new Jefferson Memorial. (You can see a rare photo of the display at the start of this chapter.)[15] By late 1944, the Declaration had returned once again to the Library of Congress in Washington, DC.[16]

Near the end of the 1940s, more than three million Americans flocked to see Jefferson's rough draft of the Declaration put on display in the "Freedom Train," a patriotic exhibit that traversed the country on rails from September 1947 to late January 1949.[17]

In 1952, the official version of the Declaration was moved from the Library of Congress to be displayed with the Constitution and the Bill of Rights in the Rotunda of the National Archives, a soaring building that looks like a Greek Temple. The Declaration has been housed there ever since. Since the opening of that display, millions of Americans have viewed the now much-faded document in person. My own first glimpse of the Declaration came during a visit to the Rotunda with my parents and sisters in a pre-bicentennial trip in 1975. My most recent glimpse of the document came when my wife and I took our young adult children to see the Declaration in 2023.

The Declaration has remained ingrained in the popular imagination thanks to America's news media, its politicians, and its entertainers. Since 1776, the phrase "all men are created equal" has appeared in American newspapers more than 330,000 times.[18] American presidents as varied in their politics as Calvin Coolidge[19] and Barack Obama[20] have extolled the Declaration.

In Frank Capra's iconic 1939 film *Mr. Smith Goes to Washington*, Senator Jefferson Smith (played by Jimmy Stewart) reads from the Declaration on the Senate floor.[21] In 1942, Capra featured the Declaration in his Oscar-winning documentary *Prelude to War* to explain why America should fight totalitarianism.[22] In 1953, Walt Disney released a short animated film titled *Ben and Me*, the climax of which focused on the Declaration of Independence.[23]

In 1966, entrepreneur Walter Knott opened a full-scale replica of Independence Hall at his Knott's Berry Farm theme park.[24] The attraction included a patriotic audio show that dramatized the debates that produced the Declaration. It still runs.

At the end of the 1960s, the Broadway musical *1776* set the story of the writing of the Declaration of Independence to song. Later, in 1972, it was produced as a feature film.[25] In September 1985, nearly fifteen million American households watched the season opener of the television series *Scarecrow and Mrs. King*, which featured a plot by terrorists to steal the Declaration from the National Archives.[26] Nearly two decades later, Disney produced the big-screen adventure *National Treasure* (2004), which told another story about a plot to steal the Declaration. It was among the top-grossing films of the year.[27]

Notwithstanding its continuing prominence in American culture, the Declaration has also provoked fierce opposition over the years—so much so that if its signers came back from the dead for a visit today, they might find large parts of America's governmental system unrecognizable.

At the time it was written, the Declaration drew support for its ideas from the Bible, philosophy, and even natural science.[28] But within a few decades, new ideas came to the forefront in America that led to a frontal assault on the Declaration's vision of equality, liberty, unalienable rights, and limited government under God. As we shall see, much of this assault was waged in the name of "science," especially Darwinian biology.

According to many of the Declaration's critics, science now proved unequivocally that humans were *not* equal. Nor were they created by God or endowed by Him with unalienable rights. Humans evolved through an unguided process, and any rights they possessed were said to have been invented by those who had sufficient power to enforce them. These rights lasted only so long as those in power were willing to grant them. Moreover, because humans were fundamentally unequal, the superior should not be required to gain the consent of the inferior. The masses should be ruled instead by elites who knew best, in the name of science.

The steady drumbeat of criticisms against the truths expressed in the Declaration has taken its toll. As America celebrates the

Declaration's 250th anniversary, many Americans are ignorant of its meaning or ambivalent about its teachings. To be sure, according to a national survey commissioned for the writing of this book, eight in ten Americans still affirm the truth of the Declaration's propositions about life, liberty, and equality;[29] however, fewer than four in ten Americans accept the Declaration's view of the source of our rights. Fewer still accept its understanding of the purposes and limits of government.

Moreover, many among America's elites—on both left and right—seem to have turned against the Declaration and the American Founding. According to left-wing journalist Nikole Hannah-Jones, the ideals of the Declaration were a "lie" because the Founders didn't apply them to enslaved blacks.[30] According to right-wing political writer Curtis Yarvin (a self-proclaimed "radical *monarchist*"[31]), the American Revolution is a story "in which evil triumphed over good"[32] and the idea that humans are born or created equal has been soundly refuted by science. Indeed, "it's hard to imagine a more thoroughly falsified scientific hypothesis."[33]

Yarvin is an unrepentant atheist, but some Christians harbor their own reservations about the Declaration. Catholic thinker Patrick Deneen writes dismissively of "calls to devotion to the abstractions of the Declaration and the Constitution,"[34] arguing that both documents were informed by "Enlightenment and liberal philosophies that... posited the existence of radically autonomous human beings in the 'state of nature.'"[35] Evangelical Christian thinker Vishal Mangalwadi believes the Declaration embodied a "fundamental mistake" that led to the French Revolution's "reign of terror."[36]

Despite the growing chorus of dissenters, I believe the Declaration's principles remain acutely relevant for today—if we are willing to heed them. But before we can follow the Declaration, we must first understand it. And to do that, we need to rescue the Declaration from the accumulated debris piled atop it by those who want to bury its truths.

I invite you to join me on a journey in the pages that follow, through the past and present and into the future. We will investigate the original meaning of the Declaration of Independence and consider how its propositions drew support from both the Bible and the science of its day. We will uncover how Darwinism and similar ideologies were employed to undermine the Declaration in the name of science, overturning its teaching on equality, subverting its understanding of liberty, and justifying the creation of a technocratic state that regulates us from cradle to grave. Finally, we will look at how new discoveries in science are actually pointing us back to the hallowed truths expressed by the Declaration—and why this matters.

More than a decade after the Declaration, America's Founders implemented their vision of good government by drafting the Constitution of 1787. Afterward, Elizabeth Powel of Philadelphia reportedly asked Benjamin Franklin what sort of government had been established. "A republic," he replied, and famously added a warning: "if you can keep it."[37]

Two-and-a-half centuries after the Declaration, Franklin's warning is perhaps more pertinent than ever. Many of us look at the current political and social landscape and we fear for the future of America. Our constitutional system is under stress. The ties of faith, family, and culture that used to bind us are fraying. So what can we do?

When a wrong turn has been made, sometimes going back is the best way forward.

If we want to restore America to health, we need to relearn the creed that helped make America great in the first place.

Gallery

The Declaration Through History

In CONGRESS, July 4, 1776.

A DECLARATION

By the REPRESENTATIVES of the

UNITED STATES OF AMERICA,

In GENERAL CONGRESS assembled.

WHEN in the Course of human Events, it becomes necessary for one People to dissolve the Political Bands which have connected them with another, and to assume among the Powers of the Earth, the separate and equal Station to which the Laws of Nature and of Nature's God entitle them, a decent Respect to the Opinions of Mankind requires that they should declare the causes which impel them to the Separation.

We hold these Truths to be self-evident, that all Men are created equal, that they are endowed by their Creator with certain unalienable Rights, that among these are Life, Liberty, and the Pursuit of Happiness—That to secure these Rights, Governments are instituted among Men, deriving their just Powers from the Consent of the Governed, that whenever any Form of Government becomes destructive of these Ends, it is the Right of the People to alter or to abolish it, and to institute new Government, laying its Foundation on such Principles, and organizing its Powers in such Form, as to them shall seem most likely to effect their Safety and Happiness. Prudence, indeed, will dictate that Governments long established should not be changed for light and transient Causes; and accordingly all Experience hath shewn, that Mankind are more disposed to suffer, while Evils are sufferable, than to right themselves by abolishing the Forms to which they are accustomed. But when a long Train of Abuses and Usurpations, pursuing invariably the same Object, evinces a Design to reduce them under absolute Despotism, it is their Right, it is their Duty, to throw off such Government, and to provide new Guards for their future Security. Such has been the patient Sufferance of these Colonies; and such is now the Necessity which constrains them to alter their former Systems of Government. The History of the present King of Great-Britain is a History of repeated Injuries and Usurpations, all having in direct Object the Establishment of an absolute Tyranny over these States. To prove this, let Facts be submitted to a candid World.

He has refused his Assent to Laws, the most wholesome and necessary for the public Good.

He has forbidden his Governors to pass Laws of immediate and pressing Importance, unless suspended in their Operation till his Assent should be obtained; and when so suspended, he has utterly neglected to attend to them.

He has refused to pass other Laws for the Accommodation of large Districts of People, unless those People would relinquish the Right of Representation in the Legislature, a Right inestimable to them, and formidable to Tyrants only.

He has called together Legislative Bodies at Places unusual, uncomfortable, and distant from the Depository of their public Records, for the sole Purpose of fatiguing them into Compliance with his Measures.

He has dissolved Representative Houses repeatedly, for opposing with manly Firmness his Invasions on the Rights of the People.

He has refused for a long Time, after such Dissolutions, to cause others to be elected; whereby the Legislative Powers, incapable of Annihilation, have returned to the People at large for their exercise; the State remaining in the mean time exposed to all the Dangers of Invasion from without, and Convulsions within.

He has endeavoured to prevent the Population of these States; for that Purpose obstructing the Laws for Naturalization of Foreigners; refusing to pass others to encourage their Migrations hither, and raising the Conditions of new Appropriations of Lands.

He has obstructed the Administration of Justice, by refusing his Assent to Laws for establishing Judiciary Powers.

He has made Judges dependent on his Will alone, for the Tenure of their Offices, and the Amount and Payment of their Salaries.

He has erected a Multitude of new Offices, and sent hither Swarms of Officers to harrass our People, and eat out their Substance.

He has kept among us, in Times of Peace, Standing Armies, without the consent of our Legislatures.

He has affected to render the Military independent of and superior to the Civil Power.

He has combined with others to subject us to a Jurisdiction foreign to our Constitution, and unacknowledged by our Laws; giving his Assent to their Acts of pretended Legislation:

For quartering large Bodies of Armed Troops among us:

For protecting them, by a mock Trial, from Punishment for any Murders which they should commit on the Inhabitants of these States:

For cutting off our Trade with all Parts of the World:

For imposing Taxes on us without our Consent:

For depriving us, in many Cases, of the Benefits of Trial by Jury:

For transporting us beyond Seas to be tried for pretended Offences:

For abolishing the free System of English Laws in a neighbouring Province, establishing therein an arbitrary Government, and enlarging its Boundaries, so as to render it at once an Example and fit Instrument for introducing the same absolute Rule into these Colonies:

For taking away our Charters, abolishing our most valuable Laws, and altering fundamentally the Forms of our Governments:

For suspending our own Legislatures, and declaring themselves invested with Power to legislate for us in all Cases whatsoever.

He has abdicated Government here, by declaring us out of his Protection and waging War against us.

He has plundered our Seas, ravaged our Coasts, burnt our Towns, and destroyed the Lives of our People.

He is, at this Time, transporting large Armies of foreign Mercenaries to compleat the Works of Death, Desolation, and Tyranny, already begun with circumstances of Cruelty and Perfidy, scarcely paralleled in the most barbarous Ages, and totally unworthy the Head of a civilized Nation.

He has constrained our fellow Citizens taken Captive on the high Seas to bear Arms against their Country, to become the Executioners of their Friends and Brethren, or to fall themselves by their Hands.

He has excited domestic Insurrections amongst us, and has endeavoured to bring on the Inhabitants of our Frontiers, the merciless Indian Savages, whose known Rule of Warfare, is an undistinguished Destruction, of all Ages, Sexes and Conditions.

In every stage of these Oppressions we have Petitioned for Redress in the most humble Terms: Our repeated Petitions have been answered only by repeated Injury. A Prince, whose Character is thus marked by every act which may define a Tyrant, is unfit to be the Ruler of a free People.

Nor have we been wanting in Attentions to our British Brethren. We have warned them from Time to Time of Attempts by their Legislature to extend an unwarrantable Jurisdiction over us. We have reminded them of the Circumstances of our Emigration and Settlement here. We have appealed to their native Justice and Magnanimity, and we have conjured them by the Ties of our common Kindred to disavow these Usurpations, which, would inevitably interrupt our Connections and Correspondence. They too have been deaf to the Voice of Justice and of Consanguinity. We must, therefore, acquiesce in the Necessity, which denounces our Separation, and hold them, as we hold the rest of Mankind, Enemies in War, in Peace, Friends.

We, therefore, the Representatives of the UNITED STATES OF AMERICA, in General Congress, Assembled, appealing to the Supreme Judge of the World for the Rectitude of our Intentions, do, in the Name, and by Authority of the good People of these Colonies, solemnly Publish and Declare, That these United Colonies are, and of Right ought to be, Free and Independent States; that they are absolved from all Allegiance to the British Crown, and that all political Connection between them and the State of Great-Britain, is and ought to be totally dissolved; and that as Free and Independent States, they have full Power to levy War, conclude Peace, contract Alliances, establish Commerce, and to do all other Acts and Things which Independent States may of right do. And for the support of this Declaration, with a firm Reliance on the Protection of divine Providence, we mutually pledge to each other our Lives, our Fortunes, and our sacred Honor.

Signed by Order *and in* Behalf *of the* Congress,

JOHN HANCOCK, President.

Attest.
CHARLES THOMSON, Secretary.

Philadelphia: Printed by John Dunlap.

Figure 1.2. The "Dunlap Broadside," the first printed version of the Declaration of Independence, July 1776, printed by John Dunlap of Philadelphia.

Figure 1.3. *Clockwise from the top:* Public readings of the Declaration of Independence in Philadelphia, Boston, and New York in July 1776.

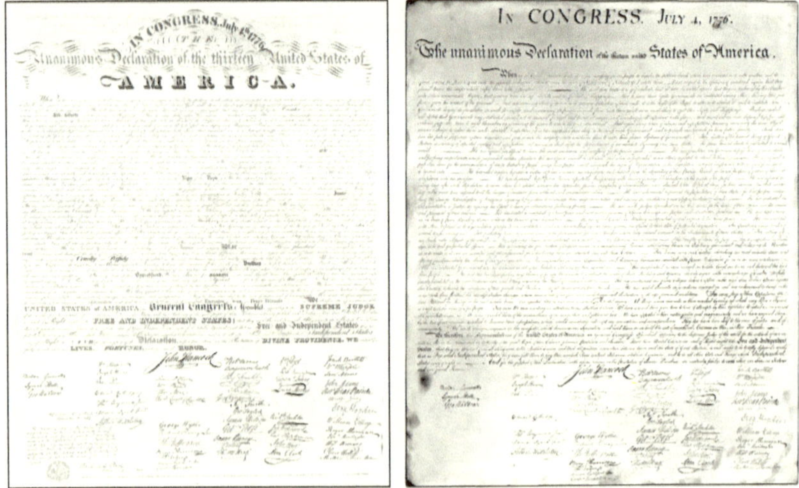

Figure 1.4. *Top:* Asher Durand's engraving (1823) of John Trumbull's iconic painting "The Declaration of Independence," which depicts the presentation of the draft Declaration to the Continental Congress. *Second row, left:* One of the earliest known decorative reproductions of the original Declaration of Independence, 1818. *Second row, right:* Copperplate engraving of the original Declaration of Independence commissioned by John Quincy Adams, 1823.

Figure 1.5. *Top*: Reading of the Declaration of Independence at Independence Hall in Philadelphia on July 4, 1876, by Richard Henry Lee, grandson of signer of the Declaration of same name. *Bottom*: Chamber in Independence Hall where the Declaration was adopted by the Continental Congress, as it appeared in 1876. The original Declaration was put on display in this room in a special safe from early 1876 to early 1877.

Figure 1.6. Librarian of Congress Herbert Putnam installing the Declaration of Independence in its new display case at the Library of Congress, February 1924.

Figure 1.7. President and Mrs. Coolidge at the dedication of the public display of the Declaration of Independence and the Constitution in the Great Hall of the Library of Congress, February 28, 1924.

Figure 1.8. Publicity materials from Frank Capra's *Mr. Smith Goes to Washington* (1939). In the film, Senator Jeff Smith (played by James Stewart) visits the Declaration at the Library of Congress and later reads from the Declaration during his filibuster on the Senate floor.

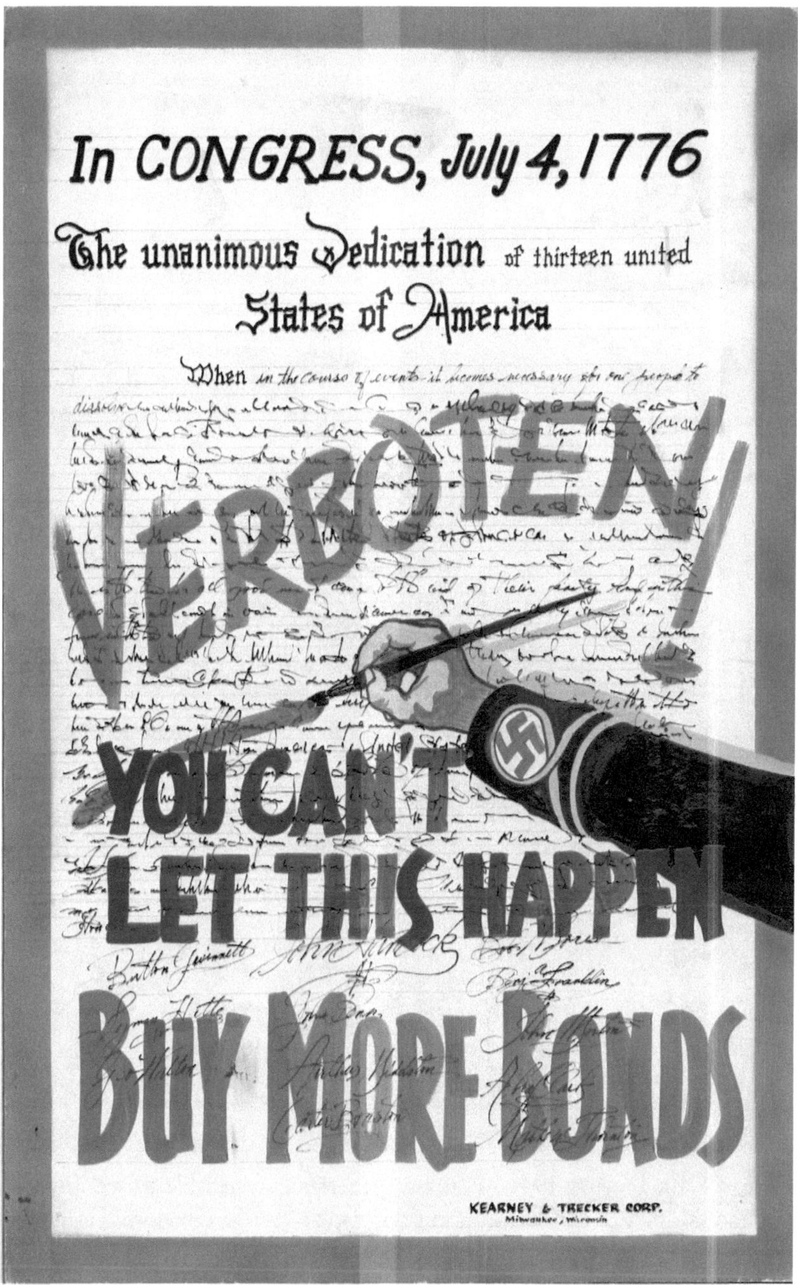

Figure 1.9. The Declaration of Independence featured in World War II poster to sell war bonds, 1940s.

Figure 1.10. During 1947-49, many Americans were able to see Thomas Jefferson's draft of the Declaration on display in the Freedom Train that traversed the country.

Figure 1.11. Transfer of the Declaration of Independence and other "Charters of Freedom" from the Library of Congress to the National Archives, and installation of the Declaration in its new exhibit case, December 1952.

Figure 1.12. *Top:* President Truman participates in the unveiling of the new Charters of Freedom exhibit at the National Archives, featuring the Declaration, the Constitution, and the Bill of Rights, December 1952. *Bottom:* Congressman (later President) Gerald Ford shows constituents the Declaration of Independence at the National Archives in July 1955.

Figure 1.13. Full-scale reproduction of Independence Hall built by entrepreneur Walter Knott for Knott's Berry Farm in California. Opened on July 4, 1966, it features a special audio-visual presentation in the recreated chamber where the Declaration was drafted.

Figure 1.14. Poster and publicity photo for *National Treasure* (2004), which features a plot to steal the original Declaration of Independence.

A Declaration by the Representatives of the UNITED STATES OF AMERICA, in General Congress assembled.

When in the course of human events it becomes necessary for one people to dissolve the political bands which have connected them with another, and to assume among the powers of the earth the separate and equal station to which the laws of nature & of nature's god entitle them, a decent respect to the opinions of mankind requires that they should declare the causes which impel them to the separation.

We hold these truths to be self-evident; that all men are created equal; that they are endowed by their creator with inherent & inalienable rights; that among these are life, liberty, & the pursuit of happiness; that to secure these rights, governments are instituted among men, deriving their just powers from the consent of the governed; that whenever any form of government becomes destructive of these ends, it is the right of the people to alter or to abolish it, & to institute new government, laying it's foundation on such principles & organising it's powers in such form, as to them shall seem most likely to effect their safety & happiness. prudence indeed will dictate that governments long established should not be changed for light & transient causes: and accordingly all experience hath shewn that mankind are more disposed to suffer while evils are sufferable, than to right themselves by abolishing the forms to which they are accustomed. but when a long train of abuses & usurpations [begun at a distinguished period &] pursuing invariably the same object, evinces a design to reduce them under absolute Despotism, it is their right, it is their duty, to throw off such government, & to provide new guards for their future security. such has been the patient sufferance of these colonies; & such is now the necessity which constrains them to [expunge] their former systems of government. the history of the present king of Great Britain is a history of [unremitting] injuries and usurpations, [among which, appears no solitary fact to contradict the uniform tenor of the rest, but all have] in direct object the establishment of an absolute tyranny over these states. to prove this, let facts be submitted to a candid world, [for the truth of which we pledge a faith yet unsullied by falsehood]

Figure 2.1. Draft of the Declaration of Independence in the hand of Thomas Jefferson.

2. We Hold These Truths

When I was in sixth grade, the principal came to our class one day to talk about a boy who was a member of the class. This boy had a hard time getting along with others, and he had difficulty controlling his outbursts. The principal said that we are told that all people are created equal, but they aren't. Some, like this boy, were broken.

I think the principal was trying to be compassionate in telling us this. He wanted to encourage us to treat our classmate with kindness and understanding.

But in retrospect, I think his comments were demeaning. And they betrayed a significant misunderstanding of what America's Founders meant by their statement "all men are created equal."

For over a decade, I taught the Declaration of Independence to college undergraduates in my freshman-level American government class. During that time, I was struck by two things: first, how earnest my students were in wanting to believe in the ideals of the Declaration; second, how many of them really didn't understand the truths proclaimed there.

The purpose of this chapter is to unpack the real meaning of the Declaration's exalted phrases and to trace their roots in both the biblical tradition and the natural philosophy (i.e., the science) of the Founding era.

"The Laws of Nature and of Nature's God"

Before we get to the most famous passage in the Declaration, there is a phrase in the document's first sentence worth pausing over. Most people probably pass over it without thinking much about it. The phrase is "the Laws of Nature and of Nature's God."

This phrase is important because it provides crucial background for understanding the rest of the Declaration. The words echo British Enlightenment thinker John Locke (1632–1704), who used the phrase "the laws of God and nature" in his *Two Treatises of Government*.[1] Locke in turn was drawing on a larger intellectual tradition. Anglican theologian Richard Hooker (1554–1600) previously employed the phrase "the law of God, and the law of nature" in his treatise *Of the Laws of Ecclesiastical Polity*.[2] Hooker in turn was quoting from the great medieval Catholic theologian Thomas Aquinas (1225–1274).[3] For his part, Jefferson made clear that the Declaration reflected ideas not only from Locke but from Aristotle, Cicero, Algernon Sidney, and others.[4] "The object of the Declaration," he wrote, was "not to find out new principles, or new arguments, never before thought of... but to place before mankind the common sense of the subject."

The "Laws of Nature" are those truths about reality that all well-formed human beings have access to through observation, reason, and conscience. The Founders weren't primarily referring here to the laws of *physical* nature (for example, the law of gravity). Instead, they had in mind the laws of *human* nature, especially the laws of morality.

The second half of the phrase—the "Laws... of Nature's God"—points to the Founders' conviction that the laws of human nature ultimately derive their authority from God himself. It also hints that humans have access to these laws not just through reason and conscience, but also through God's special revelation to us—the Bible.

In the words of Founding Father James Wilson, God's law for human beings "is communicated to us by reason and conscience, the divine monitors within us, and by the sacred oracles [i.e., the books of the Bible], the divine monitors without us."[5] A signer of both the Declaration and the Constitution, Wilson later became a Justice of the Supreme Court and was perhaps the most gifted legal theorist among the Founders. His inaugural law lecture at the College of Philadelphia was attended by luminaries such as George Washington, John Adams, and Thomas Jefferson.

The idea that reason and revelation point to the same fundamental truths about humanity was widely shared among the Founding generation. In fact, it so permeated the Founding era that the modern reader may miss it because authors of the period more often assumed this proposition than demonstrated it. When citing authority for fundamental propositions, writers of the era appealed to both reason and revelation as a matter of course. George Washington appealed to "Reason, Religion, and Philosophy,"[6] "religion, decency, and order,"[7] and "Prudence, Policy, and a true Christian Spirit."[8] John Adams appealed to "revelation, and... reason too,"[9] "the bible and common sense,"[10] "human nature and the christian religion,"[11] and "God and Nature."[12] John Jay cited "experience and revelation."[13] James Madison invoked "reason and the principles of the Xn [i.e., Christian] religion."[14] Alexander Hamilton noted that the moral doctrines of the infamous materialist philosopher Thomas Hobbes were "absurd" [i.e., against reason] as well as "impious" [i.e., against revelation].[15] Even deist and rationalist Thomas Jefferson saw fit to appeal to the "obligation of the moral precepts of Jesus"[16] as coincident with the morality of conscience and reason.

This view that reason and conscience as well as the Bible point in the same direction was not the invention of a secular age of "Enlightenment." It had deep roots in both the Bible and Christian theology.

In Romans 2:14–15, the Apostle Paul wrote about how the Gentiles were accountable to the moral law even though they did not have the law of Moses, because the dictates of the moral law were "written on their hearts, while their conscience also bears witness, and their conflicting thoughts accuse or even excuse them."[17]

Subsequent Christian thinkers embraced the same view. Augustine (354–430) wrote that "the hand of our Maker in our very hearts has written this truth: That thing which you would not do to yourself, do not do to another. No one was ignorant of this truth even before the Law of Moses was given, so that there might be some rule by which even those without the Law might be judged."[18] Thomas

Aquinas invoked Romans 2:14–15 to argue that humans have access to the principles of morality through "the natural law" as well as the Bible.[19] Martin Luther likewise cited Romans 2 to argue that the moral law given by Moses in the Ten Commandments is implanted in human beings "by nature": "For what God has given the Jews from heaven, he has also written in the hearts of all men."[20] John Calvin agreed, writing that "the law of God which we call moral, is nothing else than the testimony of natural law, and of that conscience which God has engraven on the minds of men."[21] In the twentieth century, C. S. Lewis made a similar argument in his books *Mere Christianity* and *The Abolition of Man*.[22]

This idea that reason, conscience, and revelation converge on the same truths undergirds many of the key teachings in the Declaration of Independence, including the very next phrase we will unpack.

"We Hold These Truths to Be Self-Evident"

The Declaration claims that it will enumerate certain truths that are "self-evident." Unfortunately, that very claim has been anything but self-evident to many people, and there have been continuing debates over whether the truths announced in the Declaration are truly "self-evident."

In its technical sense, a self-evident truth is a foundational proposition that you grasp as true once you understand it. For example, if you understand what a "whole" is and what a "part" is, you should grasp immediately that the whole is greater than one of its parts. Or if you understand that a = b and b = c, you should know instantly that a = c. Founder James Wilson pointed out that all disciplines have their own first principles, even moral reasoning.[23] Self-evident truths provide the foundation for all additional reasoning in a discipline. "In disquisitions of every kind there are certain primary truths, or first principles, upon which all subsequent reasonings must depend," wrote Alexander Hamilton.[24] If nothing is self-evident, there is nothing to reason about.

According to this strict definition, it's pretty clear that at least some of the things the Declaration names as self-evident truths aren't. They aren't self-contained propositions that you simply grasp as true once you understand them. They depend on other arguments and evidence to make clear their truth.

But the term "self-evident" is also used in a non-technical sense to refer to statements that are plainly true to most people, even if they aren't "self-evident" in the technical sense.[25] That seems to be how the term is being employed here.

Some note in addition that the Declaration doesn't actually claim that the truths it is proclaiming *are* self-evident.[26] What it says is "We *hold* these truths to be self-evident." Just like mathematics or morality, a political system requires a set of first principles to build upon. The Declaration seems to be arguing that there are certain crucial truths that Americans should treat as first principles in order to build their political system.

Seen in this light, whether those first principles are actually self-evident in a technical sense is not key. What *is* important is that those principles are true and provide the foundation for our political system.

Some Christians don't like the Declaration's claim of "self-evident truths." They point out that in Thomas Jefferson's original draft, the Declaration stated, "We hold these truths to be sacred and undeniable," not "self-evident." A couple of years ago, I spoke at a conference where Christian thinker Vishal Mangalwadi argued that Jefferson's original language correctly founded our government on the truths of "sacred scripture," rather than the "self-evident" truths of secular reason.[27] Mangalwadi then insisted that deist Benjamin Franklin "pushed the Founders to change the terminology, and this was not a semantic change." He "put pressure to drop the idea that, 'We hold these truths to be sacred, derived from sacred scriptures,' and say, 'We hold these truths to be self-evident, meaning derived from common sense.'"

Some secularists agree with this account of what happened, but they think it was a good thing. Atheist scientist Massimo Pigliucci lauds Franklin for transforming the Declaration from a religious document to a secular one: "With a few strokes of his pen, he transformed Jefferson's religious appeal into a statement of rational self-evidence—a change that would echo through centuries of American thought and governance."[28]

In Mangalwadi's view, the Declaration's change of wording "was the fundamental mistake" of the American Founding, a mistake that unleashed the horrors of the French Revolution. "If [the] French Revolution, which was fighting for equality, liberty, fraternity, became a reign of terror, the guilt is on [the] American Revolution," he asserted.[29] The Declaration of Independence "misled the French revolutionaries" into thinking they could have "equality, liberty, fraternity without revelation."

However, this account of the addition of "self-evident" to the Declaration is misguided, for several reasons.

First, we don't actually know who changed the Declaration's phrasing from "sacred and undeniable" to "self-evident." Journalist Walter Isaacson popularized the claim that it was Franklin simply by asserting it,[30] but scholars are divided on the question.[31] Some think Jefferson himself made the change. The reality is we don't have sufficient information to decide the question. Neither Jefferson nor Franklin nor anyone else involved in the drafting of the Declaration claimed credit for this particular change of phrasing. We do have Jefferson's rough draft of the Declaration where "sacred and undeniable" is crossed out and replaced with "self-evident," but there is no agreement on whose handwriting made the change. Princeton historian Julian Boyd, editor of *The Papers of Thomas Jefferson*, thought it was Jefferson's, not Franklin's.[32]

Second, whoever changed the original wording, there is no evidence they intended any significant change in meaning. Jefferson, Franklin, and Adams all rejected orthodox Christianity (especially the doctrine of the Trinity), and they all had a high view of human reason.[33] None of them—least of all Jefferson—would have claimed that truth can only be known as a religious proposition from the Bible. So whatever the original phrasing meant, it wasn't that the founding propositions of America were based solely on the Bible. Moreover, Jefferson later stated that the alterations suggested by Franklin and Adams "were two or three only, and merely verbal."[34] That is, they weren't substantive changes in meaning. So even if Franklin was the one who suggested the change, the whole notion that re-phrasing "sacred and undeniable" somehow represented an intention to replace Christian revelation as the sole foundation of knowledge is hard to sustain.

Third, although Jefferson, Franklin, and Adams rejected orthodox Christianity, most members of the Continental Congress did not. They were conventional or even devout Christians, including Anglicans, Presbyterians, Congregationalists, Quakers, and a Catholic.[35] They also were not reticent to speak up when they disagreed with something. The full Continental Congress made dozens of changes to various parts of the Declaration before it was finalized.[36] If any of the Christian members of Congress worried that the Bible was being displaced by secular reason in the Declaration, they would have objected and amended it. This includes Roger Sherman from Connecticut. A devout congregationalist active in church affairs,[37] Sherman served on the drafting committee for the Declaration along with Jefferson, Franklin, Adams, and Robert Livingston. Surely he would have complained if he thought the wording was somehow anti-Christian.

Finally, and most important of all, the attempt to draw a sharp distinction between "sacred and undeniable" and "self-evident" is misplaced. As we've already seen, the Founding generation thought that reason and revelation converged on the same truths. In line with the dominant Christian intellectual tradition, they did not view the Bible and human reason as in conflict.

One of the notable signers of the Declaration was the Rev. John Witherspoon, a Presbyterian minister who was president of what is now known as Princeton University. In his *Lectures on Moral Philosophy*, Witherspoon taught that "we must distinguish… between the light of nature and the law of nature: by the first is to be understood what we can or do discover by our own powers, without revelation or tradition: by the second, that which, when discovered, can be made appear to be agreeable to reason and nature."[38] According to Witherspoon, even if there are truths about morality or human behavior that can only be discovered through the Bible or tradition, those things may be shown to be "consonant to reason, or may be proven by reason" after their initial discovery.

Reason and revelation were not antagonists in the view of America's Founding generation. They were equally given to us by God, and when properly used, they both pointed to the same truths. The Declaration does not claim otherwise. Instead, it proclaims that America's political system will be based on key truths about human nature that it goes on to identify, and that regardless of how those truths are ascertained (whether through reason or revelation), they are to be held by Americans as "self-evident"—that is, they are to be regarded as foundational principles on which our government rests.

"All Men Are Created Equal"

Without question, the most widely celebrated statement in the Declaration is, "All men are created equal." This majestic proclamation has inspired generations of Americans. Yet the claim is also the most hotly disputed statement in the Declaration, and likely the most misunderstood. Seventy-eight percent of Americans still say they believe that all human beings are created equal.[39] But it's not clear that all of them understand what they are saying.[40]

They're in good company. Charles Adams was a son of John Adams, who signed and helped draft the Declaration. But even Charles struggled to understand how anyone could believe that "all men are... equal." Perhaps, he wrote his father, there could be truth to the statement "in a State of Nature," "but how any man of reflection can hold up the idea as it relates to a state of Society" was beyond him.[41]

Responding to Charles, John Adams did not disagree that humans were unequal in a variety of ways. Indeed, he wrote that "the Physical Inequalities among Men in a State of Nature are infinite."[42] They "are so obvious so determinate and so unalterable, that no Man is absurd enough to deny them." These inequalities included "inequalities of Health, Strength, Beauty, Joy, sorrow, Gaiety, Horror and despair," not to mention differences in "mental vigour." These inequalities, according to Adams, "lay the foundation for Inequalities of Wealth Power Influence and Importance, throughout human Life. Laws and Government have neither the Power nor the Right to change them."

John Adams could be a curmudgeon and a pessimist, but on this point he was simply conveying the common sense of the Founders. Fellow Declaration signer James Wilson opined at length on the same topic in his law lectures. "When we say, that all men are equal; we mean not to apply this equality to their virtues, their talents, their dispositions, or their acquirements," said Wilson, who went on to extol the differences among human beings as one of the great blessings of the Creator.[43] "Many are the degrees, many are the varieties of human genius, human dispositions, and human characters. One man has a turn for mechanicks; another, for architecture; one paints; a second makes poems: this excels in the arts of a military; the other, in those of civil life." These differences among humans were part of the plan of "Providence," according to Wilson.

This tells us a great deal about the inequalities the Founders recognized among human beings. But it does not tell us in what ways they regarded humans as equal.

Fortunately, Adams did not leave his son Charles—or us—in suspense. The elder Adams explained to his son that the true meaning of the doctrine of human equality was simple:

> It really means little more than that We are all of the same Species: made by the same God: possessed of Minds and Bodies alike in Essence: having all the same Reason, Passions, Affections and appetites. All Men are Men and not Beasts: Men and not Birds: Men and not Fishes. The Infant in the Womb is a Man, and not a Lyon. The Idiot even is a Man and not an Eagle—The Dwarf himself is a Man and not a Whale. The blind are Men, and not Insects, the deaf are Men and not reptiles, the dumb are Men and not Trees. All these are Men and not Angells: Men and not Vegetables &c.[44]

In another letter, Adams summarized his view of human equality even more concisely. We are all, he said, "equally Men, of like Bodies and Minds, the Work of the Same Artist, Children of the Same father, almighty."[45]

Figure 2.2. Key signers of the Declaration of Independence. *Each row, left to right, starting at the top:* Thomas Jefferson, Benjamin Franklin, John Adams, James Wilson, John Witherspoon, Benjamin Rush.

Seven Ways All Humans Are Equal

Digging more deeply, we can glean at least seven fundamental ways human beings are by nature equal according to the writings of Adams and other Founders.

First and foremost, as Adams wrote, we are all "made by the same God," "the Work of the Same Artist, Children of the Same father, almighty." More on this important truth later.

Second, humans are rational beings. We are "possessed of Minds... alike in Essence: having all the same Reason." Unlike insects or reptiles or whales, humans are capable of exercising rationality and voluntary action at a level that outstrips any other creature on Earth. As John Witherspoon observed, the "great and apparent distinction between man and the inferior animals" can be seen in the human capacity for "reason, memory," and "reflection."[46] James Wilson expressed a similar view. Calling the human mind "the noblest work of God,"[47] he noted that "the power of reasoning is frequently selected as the characteristick quality, which distinguishes the human race from the inferiour part of the creation."[48]

Wilson highlighted human language as providing evidence of the universality of the rational capacities of humans across cultures. "There are, in all languages, modes of speech, by which men signify their judgment, or give their testimony, or accept, or refuse, or command, or threaten, or supplicate, or ask information or advice, or plight their faith in promises or contracts," he wrote.[49] "If such operations were not common to mankind, we should not find, in all languages, forms of speech by which they are expressed." Our rational faculties give us the ability to choose to act or not act based upon reflection rather than brute instinct or necessity. "A puppet may make a few motions and gesticulations," Wilson exclaimed in his law lectures, "... but how unlike it is to that, which it represents!"[50]

Third, humans possess a moral sense, an ability to grasp the first principles of morality and act accordingly. "I think it must be admitted, that a sense of moral good and evil, is as really a principle of our nature, as either the gross external or reflex senses," wrote John Witherspoon.[51] "This moral sense is precisely the same thing with what, in scripture and common language, we call conscience. It is the law which our Maker has written upon our hearts."

James Wilson again pointed to language for corroboration of the moral sense: "All languages speak of a beautiful and a deformed, a right and a wrong, an agreeable and disagreeable, a good and ill, in actions, affections, and characters," he noted.[52] "All languages, therefore, suppose a moral sense, by which those qualities are perceived and distinguished."

Wilson argued that the ability to make moral judgments was spread throughout all classes of mankind: "Never was there any of the human species above the condition of an idiot, to whom all actions appeared indifferent. All feel that a certain temper, certain affections, and certain actions produce a sentiment of approbation; and that a sentiment of disapprobation is produced by the contrary temper, affections, and actions."[53] Even if some individual humans are bereft of a moral sense, that does not mean it should not be treated as a general feature of mankind, according to Thomas Jefferson, "because there is no rule without exceptions."[54] Jefferson went on to argue that

> it is false reasoning which converts exceptions into the general rule. Some men are born without the organs of sight, or of hearing, or without hands. Yet it would be wrong to say that man is born without these faculties: and sight, hearing and hands may with truth enter into the general definition of Man. The want or imperfection of the moral sense in some men, like the want or imperfection of the senses of sight and hearing in others, is no proof that it is a general characteristic of the species.[55]

Fourth, humans are uniquely fitted for religion. As John Witherspoon observed, we are distinguished from other living creatures on Earth by our "knowledge of God and a future state."[56] Only humans ask questions about God or build places of worship or seek the ultimate meaning of the universe.

Fifth, all human beings possess eternal souls as well as physical bodies. "Man is composed of a body and a soul intimately connected," pointed out James Wilson.[57] "The body… [i]n its present state… is a mansion well fitted for the temporary residence of its noble inhabitant."

But "in its renewed state, it will be endowed with the power of retaining that fitness forever."

These are all positive ways in which humans are equal. But there is a sixth way we are equal that is negative: We are all fallible and prone to corruption. "If men were angels, no government would be necessary," wrote James Madison in *Federalist Paper* No. 51.[58] Madison's implication, of course, is that men are far from angelic. That is why the Constitution created a government limited by checks and balances. "In framing a government which is to be administered by men over men," observed Madison, "the great difficulty lies in this: you must first enable the government to control the governed; and in the next place oblige it to control itself."

The Founders' distrust of human nature had deep roots in the Christian emphasis on human sinfulness, which pervaded much of American colonial history, especially in Puritan New England, where generations of children learned reading from *The New England Primer*, which began, "In Adam's Fall We sinned all."[59] One cannot read the sermons of Puritan clergy without being confronted by the darker side of human nature and its implications for limiting government power. In the words of the Rev. John Cotton, it is a necessity "that all power... on earth be limited, Church-power or other... It is counted a matter of danger to the State to limit Prerogatives; but it is a further danger, not to have them limited."[60] The Puritans' realism about human nature cast a long shadow, and historian of religion Sydney Ahlstrom did not exaggerate when he suggested that both the famed *Federalist Papers* and certain writings of John Adams "can be read as Puritan contributions to Enlightenment political theory."[61] Adams, for example, wrote that the passions of vanity, pride, selfishness, ambition, and avarice "are the same in all Men, under all forms of Simple Government, and when unchecked, produce the same effects of Fraud Violence and cruelty."[62]

One of my mentors, scholar of the American Founding *par excellence* Harry Jaffa, aptly summarized the implications of both the positive and negative aspects of human equality. He noted that they meant we should "recognize that human beings are neither beasts nor gods."[63] And this "means... that no one has a right to govern other human beings as God may be said rightfully to govern the world or as human beings may be said rightfully to govern the beasts of the field."

It's time to revisit the first kind of equality mentioned by Adams—the claim that we are all "made by the same God." This idea gave rise to a seventh critically important way human beings are equal according to America's Founders: an equality of rights. If all human beings ultimately derive from the same Creator, then our essential capacities as humans are neither accidents of history nor the gift of politicians or any other human being. They come from God himself. That means our rights to exercise those capacities come from God, and no human being can rightly deprive another of them. They are our rights by nature—that is, "natural rights."

In its most basic sense, "all men are created equal" meant to the Founders that all humans equally possess the same natural rights.

"However great the variety and inequality of men may be with regard to virtue, talents, taste, and acquirements," observed Founder James Wilson, "... there is still one aspect, in which all men in society, previous to civil government, are equal. With regard to all, there is an equality in rights and in obligations."[64]

These equal natural rights spring from the fact that God is the author of our natural capacities. "The supreme being gave existence to man, together with the means of preserving and beatifying that existence," wrote Alexander Hamilton.[65] "He endowed him with rational faculties, by the help of which, to discern and pursue such things, as were consistent with his duty and interest, and invested him with an inviolable right to personal liberty, and personal safety."

The Founders' belief in the truth of human equality was undergirded by both the Bible and the natural philosophy (science) of their age.

The Roots of Human Equality in the Bible and Science

For its part, the Bible taught that God "made of one blood all nations of men" (Acts 17:26) and all humanity descended from Adam and Eve, whom God originally "created... in his own image" (Genesis 1:27).

The Founders clearly understood the implications of the biblical account. Physician Benjamin Rush, a signer of the Declaration of Independence and a devout Christian, wrote that "this Divine Book, above all others, favors that equality among mankind... which constitute[s] the soul of republicanism."[66] Similarly, when claiming that "in civil society, previously to the institution of civil government, all men are equal," James Wilson paraphrased Acts 17:16 when he asserted, "Of one blood all nations are made; from one source the whole human race has sprung."[67] Elsewhere, Wilson quoted Genesis 1:27–28 verbatim.[68]

Even those skeptical of orthodox Christianity among the Founders embraced its teaching of equality. Unitarian John Adams wrote his son Charles that Christianity was "founded on that eternal and fundamental Principle of the Law of Nature Do as you would be done by: and Love your Neighbour as yourself. Equality, Equality is the Element of Christianity."[69] Deist Thomas Paine likewise taught that "the equal rights of man" was a "divine principle... for it has its origin from the Maker of man."[70] Paine continued:

> The Mosaic account of the creation, whether taken as divine authority, or merely historical, is full to this point, *the unity or equality of man.* The expressions admit of no controversy. "And God said, Let us make man in our own image. In the image of God created he him; male and female created he them." The distinction of sexes is pointed out, but no other distinction is even implied. If this be not divine authority, it is at least historical authority, and shews that the equality of man, so far from being a modern doctrine, is the oldest upon record.[71]

But the Founders did not think that the truths of human equality could be known only through the Bible. Nature itself proclaimed the ways in which men were equal, and we could ascertain these truths through our observation of the world around us. A few weeks before his death, Jefferson wrote a correspondent: "The general spread of the light of science has already laid open to every view the palpable truth, that the mass of mankind has not been born with saddles on their backs, nor a favored few booted and spurred, ready to ride them legitimately, by the grace of God."[72]

Jefferson did not spell out what he meant by "the light of science," and the term "science" in his day meant something broader than in our own. At the very least, Jefferson likely meant that our study of human nature showed us that humans hold in common a capacity for reason and reflection far above that of any other animal, a fact which speaks to their right to liberty. Similarly, our study of humans past and present should be able to show us the universality of human fallibility and depravity.

But more than this, Jefferson and the other American Founders were convinced that a study of the natural world could show us that all humans were the product of the same Creator.

Today many people are used to the idea that belief in a God who creates us is a subjective belief based on our personal faith. But that is not the view that prevailed throughout much of Western history, and it's definitely not the view of the Founders.

The Founders, moreover, were drawing upon a long and rich philosophical and theological tradition. More than two millennia ago, pagan thinkers such as Cicero already argued that nature supplies evidence of a Creator: "Can any sane person believe that all this array of stars and this vast celestial adornment could have been created out of atoms rushing to and fro fortuitously and at random? Or could any other being devoid of intelligence and reason have created them? Not merely did their creation postulate intelligence, but… intelligence of a high order."[73]

The Bible taught the same: "The heavens declare the glory of God; the skies proclaim the work of his hands" (Psalm 19:1, NIV) and "since the creation of the world God's invisible qualities—his eternal power and divine nature—have been clearly seen, being understood from what has been made, so that people are without excuse" (Romans 1:20, NIV).

Early Christian thinkers made similar arguments,[74] as did the Catholic and Protestant Christian thinkers of later eras. Catholic theologian Thomas Aquinas (1225–1274) argued that when "things which lack intelligence, such as natural bodies, act for an end," they show that "some intelligent being exists by whom all natural things are directed toward their end; and this being we call God."[75] Centuries later Protestant Reformer John Calvin (1509–1564) wrote that "the elegant structure of the world serv[es] us as a kind of mirror, in which we may behold God, though otherwise invisible."[76]

The rise of modern science in the sixteenth and seventeenth centuries reaffirmed this consensus rather than undercut it. Scientists and theologians, Christians and deists alike, thought that the discoveries of science were revealing further evidence of a Creator to whom we owed our lives and capacities.

Sir Isaac Newton (1642–1727), one of the greatest scientists who ever lived, declared that our "most beautiful" solar system "could only proceed from the counsel and dominion of an intelligent and powerful being"[77] and argued that "the best argument" for an omnipotent and omniscient God "is the frame of nature & chiefly the contrivance of the bodies of living creatures."[78] John Ray (1627–1705), a pioneering English botanist, wrote *The Wisdom of God Manifested in the Works of the Creation,* which underwent multiple editions and claimed, "There is... no more palpable and convincing argument of the existence of a Deity, than the admirable art and wisdom that discovers itself in the make and constitution, the order and disposition, the ends and uses of all the parts and members of this stately fabrick of heaven and earth."[79] Physician and poet Richard Blackmore (1654–1729) penned a seven-part poem "to demonstrate the Existence of a God from the Marks of Wisdom, Design, Contrivance, and the Choice of Ends and Means, which appear in the Universe."[80]

Leading theologians took a similar view. Calvin argued that "astronomy, medicine, and all the natural sciences" were "designed to illustrate" the proofs of God's existence.[81] Anglican Bishop Joseph Butler (1692–1752) argued that "to an unprejudiced mind, ten thousand thousand instances of design [in nature], cannot but prove a designer,"[82] while French Catholic Archbishop François Fénelon (1651–1715) wrote a book arguing that "All Nature shows the Existence of its Maker."[83]

The writings of Scottish philosopher Francis Hutcheson (1694–1746) were influential on American Founders such as Witherspoon and Jefferson. Hutcheson saw the evidence of intelligent causation throughout nature, from "the order, grandeur, regular dispositions and motions, of the visible world" to "the several classes of animals and vegetables [that] display in their whole frame exquisite mechanism, and regular structure, evidencing counsel, art, and contrivance for certain ends" to "the structure of our own nature and its powers."[84]

English philosopher and cleric Samuel Clarke (1675–1729) was a friend of Newton. In his book *A Demonstration of the Being and Attributes of God*, Clarke offered a full-throated argument that as natural science advanced, the case for atheism retreated. "The deeper Men inquire into Things, and the more Accurate Observations they make, and the more and greater Discoveries they find out... the stronger" the argument grows for God, he insisted.[85] Clarke wrote that if the ancient physician Galen with his crude knowledge could find evidence of intelligent design in the human body, "what would he have said, if he had known" about the latest discoveries in anatomy and medicine?[86] Similarly, if the arguments of ancient materialists like Epicurus and Lucretius "were so Poor and Inconsiderable, that even in that Infancy of Natural Philosophy, the Generality of Men contemned and despised them... [h]ow would they have been ashamed, if they had lived in these Days; when those very things, which they thought to be Faults and Blunders in the Constitution of Things, are discovered to be very useful and of exceeding Benefit to the Preservation and Well-Being of the whole?"[87] Finally, if the ancient Roman Cicero could be convinced of a Mind behind the universe from his "partial and very imperfect Knowledge in Astronomy... [w]hat wou'd He have said, if he had known the *Modern* discoveries in astronomy?"[88]

In America, Declaration signers John Witherspoon, James Wilson, Benjamin Franklin, and Thomas Jefferson all saw evidence of God in nature as well. Witherspoon explained that one way we can know God exists is by "contemplating the universe in all its parts, observing that it contains many irresistible proofs that it could not be eternal, could not be without a cause; that this cause must be intelligent."[89] According to Wilson, God formed man "with wisdom and design,"[90] and "when we view the inanimate and irrational

Figure 2.3. Key scientists, theologians, and philosophers who saw evidence of God in nature. *Each row, left to right, starting at the top:* Isaac Newton, John Ray, Bishop Joseph Butler, Archbishop François Fénelon, Samuel Clarke, Francis Hutcheson.

creation around and above us, and contemplate the beautiful order observed in all its motions and appearances; is not the supposition unnatural and improbable—that the rational and moral world should be abandoned to the frolicks of chance, or to the ravage of disorder?"[91] In other words, if the "beautiful order" exhibited by inanimate nature reflects God's design, how much more so should the rational part of creation (man) be subject to God's design and care?

Benjamin Franklin created his own private liturgy for use in worshiping God. The section on the adoration of God had him affirming that nature testifies to its Creator: "Thy Wisdom, thy Power, and thy GOODNESS are every where clearly seen; in the Air and in the Water, in the Heavens and on the Earth; Thou providest for the various winged Fowl, and the innumerable Inhabitants of the Water; Thou givest Cold and Heat, Rain and Sunshine in their Season, and to the Fruits of the Earth Increase."[92] Franklin's private liturgy also included a section where he instructed himself to read selections from the writings of John Ray, Richard Blackmore, and Archbishop Fénelon, all of whom championed the evidence of God provided by natural philosophy.[93]

Thomas Jefferson likewise believed that the discoveries of natural science provided a rational grounding for belief in God as Creator. Writing to John Adams in 1823, Jefferson declared, "I hold (without appeal to revelation) that when we take a view of the Universe, in its parts general or particular, it is impossible for the human mind not to perceive and feel a conviction of design, consummate skill, and indefinite power in every atom of its composition."[94] What was some of the evidence from nature Jefferson had in mind? He explained:

> The movements of the heavenly bodies, so exactly held in their course by the balance of centrifugal and centripetal forces, the structure of our earth itself, with its distribution of lands, waters and atmosphere, animal and vegetable bodies, examined in all their minutest particles, insects mere atoms of life, yet as perfectly organised as man or mammoth, the mineral substances, their generation and uses, it is impossible, I say, for the human mind not to believe that there is, in all this, design, cause and effect, up to an ultimate

> cause, a fabricator of all things from matter and motion, their preserver and regulator while permitted to exist in their present forms, and their regenerator into new and other forms.

Thomas Paine was not a signer of the Declaration, but he was one of the most influential pamphleteers of the American Revolution. He rejected the idea of the Bible being a supernatural revelation, but he too thought nature pointed squarely to God. "Everything we behold carries in itself the internal evidence that it did not make itself," he wrote, arguing that the evidence of design in "Creation speaketh an universal language" all can understand.[95] In his view, natural philosophy (i.e., natural science) was nothing more than "the study of the works of God, and of the power and wisdom of God in his works."

In sum, America's Founders were persuaded that the natural science of their day confirmed the biblical teaching that we were all created by the same God, which leads to the next part of the Declaration.

"All Men... Are Endowed by Their Creator with Certain Unalienable Rights"

In 2024, journalist Heidi Przybyla with *Politico* appeared on MSNBC to warn about an "extremist element of conservative Christians" and "Christian nationalists" who held frightening views. What were these terrifying views? They "believe that our rights as Americans, as all human beings, don't come from any earthly authority. They don't come from Congress. They don't come from the Supreme Court. They come from God."[96]

The idea that our most fundamental rights come from God rather than government is a bedrock proposition of the American Founding, including the Declaration of Independence.

Unfortunately, Przybyla is far from alone in exhibiting such stunning ignorance. In 2025, US Senator Tim Kaine from Virginia insisted that the idea that rights "don't come from the government, but come from the Creator—that's what the Iranian government believes... the statement that our rights do not come from our laws or our governments is extremely troubling."[97] With cultural gatekeepers like this, it is little wonder that only 38 percent of American adults now believe that our rights come from God.[98]

The Founders thought differently. In their view, the Bible, reason, and science taught that we are created by God. Therefore, our inherent capacities as human beings come not from other men, but from God, and no human can rightfully deprive his fellow man of that which God gave him. Hence the idea of "unalienable rights": Certain inherent rights are bestowed on us by God that cannot be rightfully violated by others or given away by us. John Witherspoon explained: "Rights are alienable and unalienable. The first we may, according to justice and prudence, surrender or give up by our own act; the others we may not."[99]

After announcing we are endowed by our Creator with unalienable rights, the Declaration goes on to enumerate them.

"Among These Are Life, Liberty and the Pursuit of Happiness"

The first unalienable right is life. We do not create ourselves. We owe our lives to God, not to other human beings. Therefore, other humans do not have the right to deprive us of our lives. Scottish philosopher Frances Hutcheson, whose works were influential among America's Founders, put it this way: "A direct Right over our Lives or Limbs… is not alienable to any Person; so that he might at Pleasure put us to death, or maim us."[100]

This is the right without which there can be no others. For unless you are alive, you can't have liberty or pursue happiness. Because the right to life is paramount, it is the government's first duty to protect against the unjust taking of life. That is why a government has police forces and armies—to prevent criminals and foreign invaders from taking the lives of its citizens. The right to life also means that the government should not be able to take someone's life arbitrarily without a full and fair trial by a jury of his peers. There should be no nighttime visits by agents of the KGB or the Gestapo who want to cart you off to torture or the firing squad.

Note that the right to life does not mean you can't forfeit your life by perpetrating a capital crime. Nor does it mean you can't willingly give up your life to save other people. In the words of Hutcheson, "We have indeed a Right to hazard our Lives in any good Action which is of importance to the Publick."[101] The right to life *does* mean that tyrants or mobs or your neighbors have no right to take your innocent life. It also means you don't have the right to end your own life by suicide. In the words of Founder James Wilson, "It was not by his own voluntary act that the man made his appearance upon the theatre of life; he cannot, therefore, plead the right... by his own voluntary act to make his exit. He did not make; therefore, he has no right to destroy himself."[102]

The unalienable rights to liberty and the pursuit of happiness are connected. We have a natural right to liberty in order that we can pursue our happiness. James Wilson argued that our natural liberty is grounded in the order of nature: "Nature has implanted in man the desire of his own happiness; she has inspired him with many tender affections towards others, especially in the near relations of life; she has endowed him with intellectual and with active powers; she has furnished him with a natural impulse to exercise his powers for his own happiness, and the happiness of those, for whom he entertains such tender affections."[103]

He added that "if all this be true, the undeniable consequence is, that he [man] has a right to exert those powers for the accomplishment of those purposes, in such a manner, and upon such objects, as his inclination and judgment shall direct; provided he does no injury to others; and provided some publick interests do not demand his labours. This right is natural liberty."

The right to liberty means we have the right to think for ourselves. In the words of Witherspoon, we have an unalienable right to our "own knowledge, thoughts, &c."[104] This extends to religious liberty. We have the right to worship God according to our own convictions. In the words of the Virginia Declaration of Rights, "All men are equally entitled to the free exercise of religion, according to the dictates of conscience."[105] As for work, we have the right to enjoy the fruits of our "own innocent Labour"[106] and employ our "faculties and industry" for our "own use."[107]

In other words, we have a right to live our daily lives without being micromanaged by others, including by oppressive government busybodies. In his first inaugural address, Jefferson declared that "the sum of good government" is "a wise and frugal government, which shall restrain men from injuring one another, shall leave them otherwise free to regulate their own pursuits of industry and improvement, and shall not take from the mouth of labor the bread it has earned."[108]

As Wilson and Jefferson made clear, a natural right to liberty does not mean we have a right to do absolutely anything we please no matter the harm to ourselves or others. The Founders were not moral relativists. At the time of the Founding, liberty was viewed as a golden mean between the extremes of slavery on the one hand and licentiousness on the other. It was the shared conviction of the Founders that human beings should not be enslaved by other men or by their own base passions. Properly understood, the right to liberty articulated by the Founders was the freedom to act in accordance with the "laws of nature and nature's God." It was the liberty to live where you want in your nation, organize your own affairs, worship God as your conscience dictated, and benefit from the fruits of your own labor and industry so long as you do not violate the moral law.

In the words of Simeon Howard in 1773, the state of liberty "is not a state of licentiousness, for the law of nature which bounds this liberty, forbids all injustice and wickedness, allows no man to injure another in his person or property, or to destroy his own life."[109] Similarly, Nathaniel Niles wrote in 1774 that "Perfect liberty and perfect government are perfectly harmonious, while tyranny and licentiousness are inconsistent with both."[110] And an anonymous colonial writer in 1783 maintained that although "liberty of action ought not to be abridged… [f]reedom is not to be construed [as] a liberty to do evil or detriment, even to the persons themselves."[111] Finally, the Virginia Declaration of Rights declared that the "blessings of liberty" can only be preserved "by a firm adherence to justice, moderation, temperance, frugality, and virtue."[112] The same idea continued to be expressed after the ratification of the Constitution of 1787. In his first inaugural address in 1790, George Washington emphasized the importance of teaching Americans "to discriminate the spirit of Liberty from that of licentiousness, cherishing the first, avoiding the last."[113]

As for our right to pursue "happiness," that pursuit was also understood to be bounded by the confines of the moral law. The Founding generation did not equate happiness with mere pleasure or whatever "feels good." Instead, they thought that happiness—whether of the individual or of the society—was brought about by virtuous behavior. In the words of the Massachusetts State Constitution (1780), "The happiness of a people and preservation of civil government essentially depend upon piety, religion and morality."[114] And to quote Simeon Howard once more, "God has given to every one liberty to pursue his own happiness in whatever way, and by whatever means he pleases, without asking the consent or consulting the inclination of any other man, provided he keeps within the bounds of the law of nature. Within these bounds, he may govern his actions, and dispose of his property and person, as he thinks proper."[115]

The Founders thought that religion played a key role in nurturing the virtues needed for the American republic to endure and flourish. "Of all the dispositions and habits which lead to political prosperity, Religion and morality are indispensable supports," counseled George Washington in his Farewell Address.[116] Washington added that "reason & experience both forbid us to expect that National morality can prevail in exclusion of religious principle." John Witherspoon similarly argued that "virtue and piety are inseparably connected… [and] to promote true religion is the best and most effectual way of making a virtuous and regular people."[117]

The Founding generation's emphasis on the necessity of virtue when talking about human freedom may sound strange to us today. After all, we have been trained by pop culture to think that freedom means the absence of virtually all restraints. If a man or woman wants to abandon one spouse in order to seduce someone else, that is "freedom." If people want to use porn or hire prostitutes, that is "freedom." If they want to imbibe addictive narcotics or hallucinogenics, that is "freedom." If they want to use filthy language in public, or perform a strip show, or post obscene images on social media, that is "freedom of expression."

One of Hollywood's iconic examples of authoritarianism is the American small town filled with straightlaced, judgmental prudes who attend church and live well-ordered, mundane lives. But the Founders knew that this Hollywood version of life is a lie. When I was a professor, I would sometimes ask my students which community was truly freer: A hip urban city where you can do whatever you want, but you must triple lock your doors and windows, your neighbor may be a child molester, and you have to worry about being mugged every time you go out the door? Or a small town where most people attend church, families are close-knit, and everyone leaves their doors unlocked and has no fear letting their kids run around town without supervision?

The Founders knew that you could have a free society only when the people are virtuous enough to be self-controlled—because if you can't control yourself, someone else will have to control you. Benjamin Franklin may have put it best: "Only a virtuous people are capable of freedom. As nations become corrupt and vicious, they have more need of masters."[118]

"To Secure These Rights, Governments Are Instituted Among Men, Deriving Their Just Powers from the Consent of the Governed"

Here we reach "the bottom line," so to speak. According to the Declaration, the government does not endow us with our rights. God does that. The government's role is simply to secure our God-given rights so we can flourish. That role is limited but crucial. Political theorist Lucas Morel puts it succinctly: "Rights are not self-enforcing. They need protection to be enjoyed. That's the purpose of government."[119]

Because human beings are created equal, the powers exercised by government to secure our rights require the consent of the governed in order to be just. "No one has a right to any authority over another without his consent: all lawful government is founded on the consent of those who are subject to it," wrote James Wilson.[120] No elite is so superior that its members have a right to rule over others unilaterally by virtue of their superiority. That's why, adds Harry Jaffa, "those who live under the laws should share in making them and... those who make the laws must live under them."[121]

In the Founders' view, the purpose of government was neither to create heaven on earth nor to make us all citizens of heaven. It was not to eradicate all pain and suffering, or save us from all of our mistakes, or equalize all of our incomes. The primary goal was to protect us from each other (and from oppressive government) so we would be free to pursue our own happiness within the boundaries of the laws of nature and nature's God. And because government was supposed to be based on our unchanging nature, its goals and limited powers should not evolve over time. They should remain the same.

The Founders' vision of America was constructed on the foundation of a particular understanding of humanity, one that upheld humans as equally created in the image of God and therefore capable of reason, morality, and voluntary action, even if also prone to corruption. This high but not naïve view of humans was grounded in the Bible, history, and the natural science of the day.

But even as the Founders completed their work, storm clouds were rising on the horizon.

Within a few short years, the underpinnings of the Founders' entire system came under unrelenting attack and scorn. A growing number of voices denied that human beings are created equal or that they possess unalienable rights. Many denied that humans were moral agents or that permanent moral truths even existed. They denied that government required the consent of the governed.

As we shall see, a driving force behind many of these attacks was a radically new conception of science.

Figure 3.1. Alexander H. Stephens (1812–1883), vice president of the Confederacy.

3. A Second American Revolution

A month before the inauguration of President Abraham Lincoln in March 1861, representatives from six southern states convened in Montgomery, Alabama, to draft a constitution for the new Confederate States of America. A few weeks later, the Confederacy's Vice President Alexander Stephens came to Savannah, Georgia, to extol the virtues of the new document.

"The new constitution," Stephens told his audience, was vastly superior to the US Constitution because it "has put at rest, forever, all the agitating questions relating to our peculiar institution African slavery."[1]

The US Constitution of 1787 did protect slavery "while it should last," acknowledged Stephens. But it still set up a government that rested on a falsehood. "Most of the leading statesmen at the time of the formulation of the old constitution" embraced the belief "that the enslavement of the African was in violation of the laws of nature; that it was wrong in principle, socially, morally, and politically." True, slavery "was an evil they knew not well how to deal with, but the general opinion of the men of that day was that, somehow or other in the order of Providence, the institution would be evanescent and pass away."

"Those ideas… were fundamentally wrong," declared Stephens. "They rested upon the assumption of the equality of races. This was an error. It was a sandy foundation, and the government built upon it fell when the 'storm came and the wind blew.'"

By contrast, the Confederacy's "new government is founded upon exactly the opposite idea; its foundations are laid, its corner-stone rests, upon the great truth that the negro is not equal to the white man; that slavery subordination to the superior race is his natural and normal condition." Stephens boasted that "our new government... is the first, in the history of the world, based upon this great physical, philosophical, and moral truth." He added that he could not permit himself "to doubt the ultimate success of a full recognition of this principle throughout the civilized and enlightened world."

A mere eighty-five years after the Declaration of Independence, more than five million Americans abandoned the United States to support a new government founded on the Declaration's repudiation.

What had happened?

The short answer is that there was another revolution underway in America, a revolution that was undermining the evidence used to justify the ideals of the original American Revolution. To understand the ramifications of that second revolution, we must first understand the positive implications of the original revolution.

Slavery and the American Founding

From the start, the Founders' declaration that "all men are created equal" had important implications for the equal treatment of all human beings, regardless of race or ethnicity. Some of America's Founders owned slaves, and still more exhibited prejudice toward black people. Despite this fact, these Founders acknowledged that slavery was immoral and against the natural rights possessed by all human beings.

Some might be tempted to dismiss the founding generation's criticisms of slavery as mere hypocrisy. But I think it was more than that. Over time, the ideals they embraced in their battle against England for freedom began to influence their views on slavery.[2]

Benjamin Franklin originally owned a few slaves, but he freed the last of them in 1781.[3] Near the end of his life, he denounced slavery as "an atrocious debasement of human nature"[4] and became president of the Pennsylvania Society for Promoting the Abolition of Slavery. A few months before his death, he petitioned the United States Congress on behalf of the Society to "devise means for removing" slavery from America and to stop the slave trade.[5] In his petition, Franklin argued that the number of Americans opposed to slavery had grown in the years after the Revolution as "a just & accurate Conception of the true Principles of liberty… spread through the land." According to Franklin, the truth that "mankind are all formed by the same Almighty being, alike objects of his Care & equally designed for the Enjoyment of Happiness" was taught by both Christianity and America's founding principles: "the Christian Religion teaches us to believe [it] & the Political Creed of America fully coincides with the Position."

John Jay owned several slaves, but he freed them as well.[6] A devout Christian, Jay served as president of the Continental Congress, first Chief Justice of the United States Supreme Court, and longtime president of the American Bible Society.[7] Along with Alexander Hamilton, he helped found a society in New York in 1785 for the emancipation of slaves. In 1786, Jay wrote to a correspondent that "it is much to be wished that slavery may be abolished. The honour of the States, as well as justice and humanity, in my opinion, loudly call upon them to emancipate these unhappy people."[8] Then he added the kicker: "To contend for our own liberty, and to deny that blessing to others, involves an inconsistency not to be excused." Jay understood that the principles of the Revolution had clear implications for those who had been enslaved.

At the Constitutional Convention of 1787, James Madison lamented that "we have seen the mere distinction of colour made in the most enlightened period of time, a ground of the most oppressive dominion ever exercised by man over man."[9] The same year, Englishman John Stockdale published Thomas Jefferson's book *Notes on the State of Virginia*, in which Jefferson reflected on the evils of slavery and opined: "I tremble for my country when I reflect that God is just: [and] that his justice cannot sleep for ever."[10]

Jefferson further acknowledged that "the Almighty has no attribute which can take side with" the slaveowners over those enslaved. But Jefferson saw a hopeful change in opinion wrought since the Revolution. "I think a change already perceptible, since the origin of the present revolution. The spirit of the master is abating, that of the slave rising from the dust, his condition mollifying, the way I hope preparing, under the auspices of heaven, for a total emancipation, and that this is disposed, in the order of events, to be with the consent of the masters, rather than by their extirpation."

He had some reason for hope. As the principles of the Revolution spread, so too did efforts to end slavery. Indeed, by the early 1800s twelve of the original thirteen states had banned the importation of slaves, and eight states had acted to abolish slavery itself.[11] New York passed a law that after a certain date every child born to slave parents would be born free. The date chosen for emancipation made the connection to the principles of the Declaration of Independence unmistakable: July 4, 1799.[12]

There were also efforts to stop the spread of slavery to new states. In 1787, the Confederation Congress banned slavery in the Northwest Territory, the "massive tract of land that would eventually become the states of Illinois, Indiana, Michigan, Ohio, Wisconsin, and a section of Minnesota."[13] In 1798, an attempt was even made to stop the spread of slavery into the new southern territory of Mississippi, but it couldn't muster a majority in Congress.[14]

At the same time, some Americans began advocating for basic political rights for all free inhabitants regardless of color. America's first constitution, the Articles of Confederation, declared that "the free inhabitants of each of these states… shall be entitled to all privileges and immunities of free citizens in the several states."[15] The broad wording was intentional. A representative from South Carolina proposed that the provision be changed to "free *white* inhabitants," but the amendment was voted down overwhelmingly by eight states.[16]

There also was growing recognition in the initial years after the Revolution that free blacks should have the right to vote. In a pathbreaking study of black political activism before the Civil War, historian Van Gosse points out that "in most of the original states, black men had participated in elections to ratify the Constitution."[17] In fact, as of 1789, there was "some form of black suffrage" in New

Hampshire, Massachusetts, New York, New Jersey, North Carolina, Rhode Island, Connecticut, Pennsylvania, Maryland, and Delaware. In Massachusetts, a hotbed of the Revolution, a draft constitution for the state in 1778 "was emphatically rejected" at town meetings in part because it attempted to deprive free people of color the right to vote.[18]

There were certainly many opponents to legal equality for blacks during this period, but my point is that the principles of the American Revolution—articulated most powerfully in the Declaration of Independence—nurtured a culture of change.

So what turned the tide against applying the Revolution's principles to the treatment of blacks in America, both slave and free?

An advance in technology likely played a role. The invention of the cotton gin in the 1790s made cotton farming more profitable, supplying a substantial economic incentive to perpetuate slavery and reject the truths proclaimed in the Declaration of Independence.[19]

But a change in the world of ideas also played a key role.

Alexander Stephens himself identified the change in his speech defending the Confederacy. Stephens treated the belief that all men are created equal and endowed with certain unalienable rights as an outdated superstition "clung to" by fanatics. Why was the belief outdated? Because, according to Stephens, the inferiority of blacks had now been proven by "science."

The Rise of "Scientific" Racism in America

Stephens compared the supposed discovery of black inferiority to Galileo's discoveries in astronomy, the ideas of Adam Smith in economics, and the findings of physician William Harvey about the circulation of blood. He observed that Harvey's revolutionary discoveries had been rejected by his peers, only to be accepted later by everyone as true: "It is stated that not a single one of the medical profession, living at the time of the announcement of the truths made by him, admitted them. Now, they are universally acknowledged." Stephens thought the lesson of history was clear: "May we not, therefore, look with confidence to the ultimate universal acknowledgment of the truths upon which our system rests?"

According to Stephens, the Confederacy was "the first government ever instituted upon the principles in strict conformity to nature." In other words, it was the first government based squarely on discoveries in modern science said to establish the fact of inequality between whites and blacks. At the same time, Stephens invested his vision of scientific racism with all the religiosity he could muster. He insisted that the scientific revelation of intrinsic black inferiority was "in conformity with the ordinance of the Creator" and chastised those who were "attempting to make things equal which the Creator had made unequal."

The extremes to which Stephens took his advocacy of black inferiority could be seen when he identified it as the cornerstone of the new Confederate government: "This stone which was rejected by the first builders [America's Founders] 'is become the chief of the corner'—the real 'corner-stone'—in our new edifice." Stephens was blasphemously appropriating words from the New Testament where Jesus was identified as the cornerstone (Matthew 21:42, Mark 12:10, Luke 20:17, Ephesians 2:20, 1 Peter 2:6–7). Stephens replaced Jesus with the doctrine of scientific racism.

Stephens's claims seem outlandish today, and deservedly so. Yet they reflected a powerful new intellectual current of the day that had been growing for decades among philosophers and scientists.

Even as American patriots were declaring that all men are created equal and endowed with certain unalienable rights, a vanguard of intellectuals was enlisting science to supply a justification for racism by repudiating the natural unity and equality of mankind.

The Bible clearly teaches monogenism, the idea that all humans ultimately descended from one ancestral pair, Adam and Eve. Monogenism implies that all humans are equally human, at least at their point of origin. But influential new voices were now contending for polygenism, the contrary idea that different races had separate and distinct origins. And if they had separate origins, why should they be regarded as equally created in the image of God? After all, they would no longer be part of the same family related by biological descent.

Famed Scottish philosopher Lord Kames appeared to argue for polygenism in his *Sketches of the History of Man*, originally published in 1774. Kames asserted that while different varieties of horses "are of one kind," "men are not all of one kind; for if a White mix with a Black in whatever climate… the result will not be either an improvement of the kind, or the contrary, but a mongrel breed differing from both parents. It is thus ascertained beyond any rational doubt, that there are different races of kinds of men" that were separately created and not descended from the same ancestors.[20] He acknowledged that his finding seemed incompatible with the teaching of Genesis "that God created but a single pair of the human species" from which everyone else descended.[21] Kames gingerly avoided directly claiming that Genesis was false. But he came right up to the edge of doing so: "Though we cannot doubt of the authority of Moses, yet his account of the creation of man is not a little puzzling, as it seems to contradict every one of the facts mentioned above."[22]

American intellectual Samuel Stanhope Smith took issue with Kames's effort to undermine the unity of the human race. A Presbyterian minister and president of the College of New Jersey (Princeton), Smith in 1787 published *An Essay on the Causes of the Variety of Complexion and Figure in the Human Species*, which condemned the "arbitrary hypothesis that men are originally sprung from different stocks, and are therefore divided by nature into different species."[23] Smith argued that variations among humans could be explained through the normal effects of climate and culture over time.

He further argued that the denial of the essential "unity of the human species" would lead to all manner of confusion.[24] "The science of morals would be absurd; the law of nature and nations would be annihilated; no general principles of human conduct, of religion, or of policy could be framed; for human nature, originally infinitely various, and, by the changes of the world, infinitely mixed, could not be comprehended in any system. The rules which would result from the study of our own nature, would not apply to the natives of other countries who would be of different species; perhaps not to two families in our own country, who might be sprung from a dissimilar composition of species. Such principles tend to confound all science, as well as piety."[25]

In 1810, Smith published a new edition of his book. In the new version, he chastised Thomas Jefferson for speculating on the inferiority of his black slaves in *Notes on the State of Virginia*. "Genius, in order to its cultivation, and the advantageous display of its powers, requires freedom," rejoined Smith.[26] "The abject servitude of the negro in America, condemned to the drudgery of perpetual labor, cut off from every mean of improvement, conscious of his degraded state in the midst of freemen who regard him with contempt" hardly provided fair conditions for the Africans' talents to flourish.[27] Smith gave a tart response to Jefferson's patronizing dismissal of the writings of African American poetess Phillis Wheatley: "I will demand of Mr. Jefferson, or any other man who is acquainted with American planters, how many of those masters could have written poems equal to those of Phillis Wh[e]atley?"[28] Elsewhere, Smith advocated racial intermarriage as a way of breaking down the prejudices between whites and blacks.[29]

Smith's riposte to the polygenists was influential in both America and Europe. But as the nineteenth century wore on, Smith's view was increasingly marginalized as a new generation of American scientists arose who, scorning the Bible's teaching that humans descended from an original couple, pressed a vigorous case for polygenism.

Physician Samuel George Morton (1799–1851) argued for "a plurality of origins for the human species,"[30] treating his view as a divine disclosure: "*The doctrine of the original diversity of mankind unfolds itself to me more and more with the distinctness of revelation.*"[31] Morton assiduously collected and measured skulls representing different races, claiming that blacks demonstrated the smallest cranial size and therefore the smallest brains.

Swiss-born Harvard biologist Louis Agassiz (1807–1873) also repudiated the idea that "mankind originated from a common stock," calling it "an assumption for which there is no evidence whatever."[32] Agassiz argued instead that "what are called human races… are distinct primordial forms."[33] Somewhat nonsensically, he insisted that his "conclusions in no way conflict with the idea of the unity of mankind," because such unity can be based on "a typical structure, and… the similarity of natural abilities and propensities."[34] But here Agassiz was being disingenuous. For at the same time he insisted his views were consistent with the unity of mankind, he also insisted that "the differences between distinct races are often greater than those distinguishing species of animals one from the other."[35]

How so? "The chimpanzee and gorilla do not differ more one from the other than the Mandingo and the Guinea Negro: they together do not differ more from the orang than the Malay or white man differs from the Negro."[36] Again, "I maintain distinctly that the differences observed among the races of men are the same kind and even greater than those upon which the anthropoid monkeys are considered as distinct species." Given these views, Agassiz's claim that he still accepted the unity of the human race is hard to credit.

Ethnologists Josiah Clark Nott (1804–1873) and George Gliddon (1809–1857) were disciples of Samuel Morton, who pressed Morton's views even further. Nott portrayed the debate over polygenism as a battle royal between Science (with a capital S) and theological superstitions based on outdated interpretations of the Bible. Nott argued that "the diversity of races must be accepted by Science as a *fact*" (emphasis Nott's),[37] and he depicted the coming victory of scientific racism as the inevitable advance of science: "Scientific truth, exemplified in the annals of Astronomy, Geology, Chronology, Geographical distribution of animals, &c., has literally fought its way inch by inch through false theology. The last grand battle between science and dogmatism, on the primitive origin of races, has now commenced. It requires no prophetic eye to foresee that science must again, and finally, triumph."[38]

G. K. Chesterton was characteristically apt when he quipped that "there was *more* sympathy for the negro in the school of Jefferson than in the school of Jefferson Davis" and that the scientific proponents of racism regarded "the utter separation and subordination of the black like a beast" as "a *progress*" and as "a growth of nineteenth-century enlightenment and experiment; a triumph of science over superstition."[39]

Black abolitionist Frederick Douglass derided the new scientific racism as "scientific moonshine,"[40] lamenting that in an age of

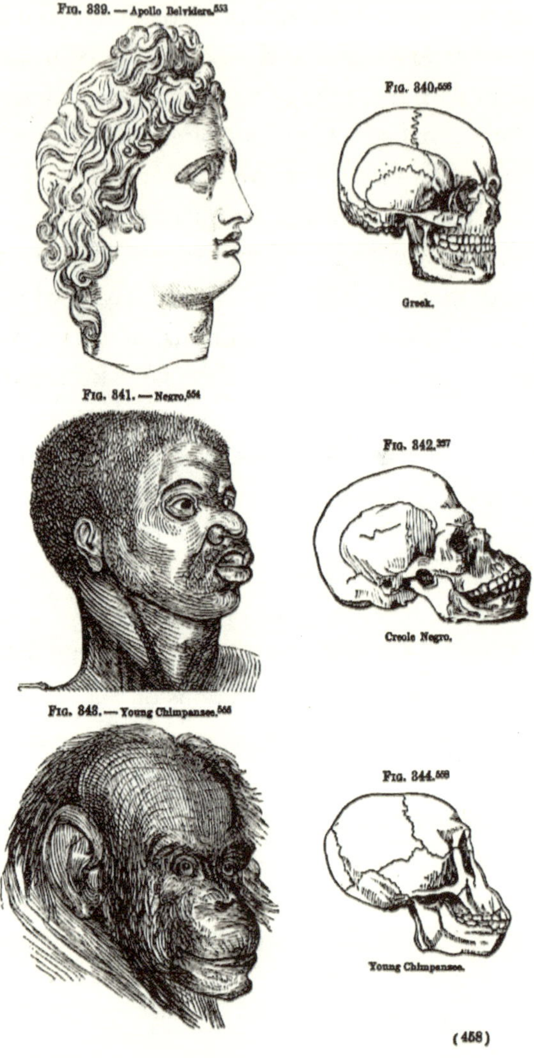

Figure 3.2. Comparison of the cranial anatomy of a European (Greek), a black man, and a chimpanzee in J. C. Nott and Geo. R. Gliddon, *Types of Mankind* (1854), 458. On the previous page Nott commented, "I belong not to those who are disposed to degrade any type of humanity to the level of the brute-creation. Nevertheless, a man must be blind not to be struck by similitudes between some of the lower races of mankind, viewed as connecting links in the animal kingdom; nor can it be rationally affirmed, that the Orang-Outan and Chimpanzee are more widely separated from certain African and Oceanic Negroes than are the latter from the Teutonic or Pelasgic types."

scientific and technological progress "there should arise a phalanx of learned men—speaking in the name of science—to forbid the magnificent reunion of mankind in one brotherhood."[41]

According to Douglass, the manhood of the black man was plain to see. "His speech, his reason, his power to acquire and to retain knowledge, his heaven-erected face, his habitudes, his hopes, his fears, his aspirations, his prophecies, plant between him and the brute creation, a distinction as eternal as it is palpable."[42]

Unfortunately, for many Americans claims made in the name of science trumped common sense.

Consider the experience of Moncure Daniel Conway of Virginia. A descendant of a signer of the Declaration of Independence, Conway grew up favoring the institution of slavery. Yet by age nineteen the injustices he saw against blacks troubled him. "Before my radical Jeffersonianism the negro stood demanding recognition as a man and a brother; else he must be treated as an inferior animal," he recalled later.[43]

Conway's ambivalence made him susceptible to Louis Agassiz and his evidence against "the unity of human species."[44] Conway was enthralled by the new gospel of separate origins because it helped him assuage his pangs of conscience about the mistreatment of blacks. He had already learned to love science in college, and Agassiz provided him with a scientific justification for slavery. Conway thereupon publicly announced at the local Lyceum "a theory that the negro was not a man within the meaning of the Declaration of Independence." The audience was shocked—not because they were anti-slavery (they weren't), but because his new theory contradicted the biblical teaching that all humans descended from Adam. Conway then set himself to defend his new scientific view:

> I sat down as wrangler of the new theory, surrounded myself with books on races, mental philosophy, and Biblical criticism, and achieved fifteen closely written letter pages to prove that mankind are not derived from one pair; that the "Caucasian" race is the highest species; and that this supreme race has the same right of dominion over the lower species of his genus that he has over quadrupeds,—the same right in kind but not in degree.[45]

For Conway, the solution Agassiz supplied to his doubts about slavery was only temporary. He later recanted and embraced abolition. And, of course, the North ultimately won the Civil War, seemingly vindicating the claims of the Declaration of Independence. Act I of the revolution against the Declaration of Independence had drawn to a close with the Declaration's ideals still embraced by many Americans. But Act II of this second revolution was already underway.

A little over a year before Alexander Stephens delivered his infamous "Cornerstone" speech, Charles Darwin had published his book *On the Origin of Species* in England. A few months later, the book came out in America.

Darwin's ideas had momentous consequences for American culture and politics, consequences we are still reeling from today. Darwinism challenged not only the Declaration's idea of human equality, but its entire philosophy of man and nature. To be sure, Darwinism was not the only source of the new challenge to the principles of the Declaration. But it was a particularly powerful one—because its challenge was made squarely in the name of *science*.

Figure 4.1. Ota Benga (c. 1883–1916), an African man from the Congo, put on public display in the primate house at the Bronx Zoo in 1906.

4. The Triumph of Scientocracy

The significance of Darwin's theory of evolution for human society is widely misunderstood today. Many seem to think the only real controversies over the theory focus on the age of the Earth or how to interpret the book of Genesis. Others claim that Darwin's theory is simply about science and has no inherent implications for culture at all.

Darwinian philosopher Daniel Dennett was more perceptive. "Darwinian theory is a scientific theory," he acknowledged, "… but that is not all it is. Darwin's dangerous idea cuts much deeper into the fabric of our most fundamental beliefs than many of its sophisticated apologists have yet admitted, even to themselves."[1] (To be clear, Dennett thought the revolutionary implications of Darwinism were a good thing.)

So what did Darwin actually advocate?

First, he proposed that all creatures, including humans, had descended with modifications from one or a few simple primordial organisms.[2]

Second, he proposed that human beings and the rest of nature were produced by a process of natural selection, or survival of the fittest, acting on random variations in nature. This two-fold mechanism that he envisioned is both blind and unguided. As Darwin made clear, it is an unintelligent process oblivious of the future. "There seems to be no more design in the variability of organic beings and in the action of natural selection," he wrote, "than in the course which the wind blows."[3]

Third, Darwin proposed that the engine of progress in the history of life is mass death. Instead of believing that the remarkable features of humans and other living things reflect the intelligent design of a master artist, Darwin portrayed death and destruction as the ultimate creator: "Thus, from the war of nature, from famine and death, the most exalted object which we are capable of conceiving, namely, the production of the higher animals, directly follows."[4]

Fourth, Darwin was committed to offering materialist explanations for the things he observed in nature. Materialism is the ancient idea that everything that exists can be fully explained as the result of blind matter in motion. Whether or not Darwin himself was a complete materialist, he did try to explain the development of life and culture in material terms. He was not alone. He lived during a period when many thinkers in the sciences were trying to offer materialist explanations for everything around us, including mind, morality, and religion. The quest to understand everything materialistically was so strong among some elites that one thinker on science in 1919 observed approvingly that "it may be said with truth that we are all materialists now."[5]

Darwin's ideas conflicted with the account of reality offered by the Declaration of Independence, and eventually they led many in America's governing classes to deny key propositions of the Declaration.

The Denial of a Creator

The Declaration of Independence is premised on the idea that both nature and the human race were intentionally created by God. As we saw in Chapter 2, the Founders regarded the existence of a Creator as not just a proposition of faith but also a truth knowable by human reason and grounded in the consensus view of science. Darwinism took a wrecking ball to that consensus.

Darwin himself was ambivalent about whether God existed, and his theory does not logically necessitate atheism. But it certainly encourages it. Think about it: If nature really supplies proof that the history of life is the product of an unguided process, then that would seem to make an atheist worldview much more credible. As Oxford University biologist Richard Dawkins famously put it, "Darwin made it possible to be an intellectually fulfilled atheist."[6] That is why so many scientists have made unguided Darwinian evolution a cornerstone in their case for atheism. Harvard evolutionary biologist E. O. Wilson declared that the existence of a God "who directs organic evolution and intervenes in human affairs... is increasingly contravened by biology and the brain sciences."[7] And by biology, he meant historical biology as viewed through the lens of evolutionary theory. University of Washington evolutionary psychologist David Barash makes a similar declaration: "The more we know of evolution, the more unavoidable is the conclusion that living things, including human beings, are produced by a natural, totally amoral process, with no indication of a benevolent, controlling creator."[8]

The impact of Darwinism and other forms of scientific materialism on the beliefs of intellectual elites as a class could be seen by the early 1900s when a survey of America's prominent biologists found that only 16.9 percent believed in God and only 25.4 percent believed in immortality. Leading physical scientists were only slightly more pious, with 34.8 percent believing in God and 40 percent believing in immortality.[9] Leading historians and sociologists showed similarly dismal results.[10] Leading psychologists were the most atheistic of all, with only 13.2 percent believing in God and 8.8 percent believing in immortality.[11]

In our own day, the corrosive impact of Darwinism on religious belief has continued. In a 2016 survey of American atheists and agnostics, nearly seven in ten atheists and more than four in ten agnostics said that Darwin's unguided mutation/natural selection mechanism made the existence of God "less likely" for them personally.[12] Similarly, more than seven in ten atheists and nearly four in ten agnostics agreed with evolutionary biologist Richard Dawkins that "the universe we observe has precisely the properties we should expect if there is, at bottom, no design, no purpose, no evil and no good, nothing but blind, pitiless indifference."[13]

But Darwinism's impact on religion is not limited to atheists and agnostics. It also has reshaped the way many Christians view God, especially at various Christian colleges and universities, where scientists and theologians have tried to revise Christianity to make it compatible with Darwinism. Because Darwinian evolution is by nature unguided, theistic Darwinists often downplay or reject the idea that God actively directs the development of life. For example, Anglican priest and physicist John Polkinghorne wrote that "an evolutionary universe is theologically understood as a creation allowed to make itself."[14] Roman Catholic biologist Kenneth Miller of Brown University insists that "mankind's appearance on this planet was *not* preordained, that we are here... as an afterthought, a minor detail, a happenstance in a history that might just as well have left us out."[15] The late Vatican astronomer George Coyne even claimed that because evolution is unguided "not even God could know... with certainty" that "human life would come to be."[16]

Other theistic Darwinists repudiate the biblical doctrine of a historic "fall," the idea that human beings were originally created good and then fell into sin through a voluntary act of disobedience. According to Christian physicist Karl Giberson, since human beings were created through Darwinian evolution, they were essentially sinful from the start because "selfishness... drives the evolutionary process."[17]

Still other theistic Darwinists challenge the idea that God's handiwork in nature, particularly in the biological realm, is observable. Christian geneticist Francis Collins suggests that "evolution could appear to us to be driven by chance, but from God's perspective the outcome would be entirely specified. Thus, God could be completely and intimately involved in the creation of all species, while from our perspective... this would appear a random and undirected process."[18] In other words, God makes the history of life look "random and undirected," even though it really is not. Contra Collins, for thousands of years Jewish and Christian thinkers believed otherwise, maintaining that God's design could be clearly seen throughout nature.[19]

The Denial of Human Equality

The Declaration of Independence proclaims that it is self-evident "that all men are created equal." As we saw in the second chapter, the Founders did not mean by this that all humans are equal in every possible way. They meant that all of us are equally human and entitled to our natural rights of life, liberty, and the pursuit of happiness. To cite again the words of Jefferson, expressed a few weeks before his death: "The general spread of the light of science has already laid open to every view the palpable truth, that the mass of mankind has not been born with saddles on their backs, nor a favored few booted and spurred, ready to ride them legitimately, by the grace of God."[20] Darwinism claimed precisely the opposite, that science has revealed that there are entire classes of humans fitted by evolution to be subjugated by their superiors.

The decisive role Darwinian theory played in solidifying scientific racism is often obscured today. Defenders of Darwin like to point out that he opposed slavery and rejected polygenism. While both facts are true, they aren't as significant as one might first think. By the time Darwin was born, the popular tide in England had already turned against slavery. Slavery had lacked legal protection for decades within England, and the slave trade had been banned throughout the British Empire.[21] And by the time Darwin was in his twenties, England had acted to end slavery itself throughout most of the Empire.[22] So Darwin's opposition to slavery was not unusual for an Englishman of his time and place in society.

As for Darwin's rejection of polygenism, it did not mean he repudiated scientific racism. Darwin did not advocate returning to biblical monogenism, with all humans descending from an original couple who had been created in God's image. Instead, he proposed that all humans ultimately evolved from original ape-like ancestors. Darwin replaced the racism of separately originated races with the racism of human groups embodying different stages of evolution. Polygenism was pushed to the fringes of science by an equally virulent Darwinian racism that soon became a respectable part of mainstream science. As Harvard evolutionary biologist Stephen Jay Gould acknowledged,

"Biological arguments for racism may have been common before 1859 [when Darwin published his book *On the Origin of Species*], but they increased by orders of magnitude following the acceptance of evolutionary theory."[23]

Darwin believed that his theory of evolution by natural selection provided a scientific explanation for why we should *expect* races to have unequal capacities and why there were "higher" and "lower" races. The specific traits an animal needs to survive differ based on the animal's environment. Thus, there is no reason to expect that natural selection acting on different populations will produce the same traits in every population or, in this case, every race.

Accordingly, Darwin declared that there are significant differences in the mental faculties of what he called "men of distinct races."[24] He also argued that the break in evolutionary history between apes and humans came "between the negro or Australian [aborigine] and the gorilla," thus depicting blacks as the closest human beings to apes.[25]

Darwin's supporters further popularized these ideas. German scientist Ernst Haeckel was a correspondent of Darwin and one of the most celebrated champions of Darwin's theory in Germany in the late nineteenth and early twentieth centuries. Haeckel created a widely disseminated diagram of human evolution that portrayed the evolutionary gap between the highest human and the lowest human as larger than the gap between the lowest human and the highest ape-like creature, which was given African features.[26]

The idea that non-white races represented a throwback to lower stages of evolution was widely embraced throughout the mainstream scientific community in the early twentieth century. Consider the views of American biologist Charles Davenport, a member of the National Academy of Sciences and regarded as one of the founding fathers of modern genetics. Davenport was obsessed with the idea that some races were still stuck in lower evolutionary stages. In his words, "It seems probable that in the same country we have, living side by side, persons of advanced mentality, persons who have inherited the mentality of their ancestors of the early Stone Age, and persons of intermediate evolutionary stages."[27]

The idea that non-white races were less evolved than whites spread to popular culture. At the St. Louis World's Fair in 1904, thousands of indigenous people from around the world were put on public display in what has become known as a "human zoo."[28] The displays were organized by distinguished anthropologist William McGee, who had served as acting president of the American Association for the Advancement of Science. McGee argued that scientists had now shown that "the structure of the lowest humans more nearly resembles that of the highest... ape-like animals... than that of the highest humans."[29] McGee was determined to use primitive peoples at the fair to dramatize for the public the different stages of human evolution—beginning with races he considered lowest on the evolutionary scale. McGee arranged for native peoples to be put on display in "villages" designed to recreate their native habitats. These villages were enclosed by fences—making them truly seem like human zoos.

Included among the displays of indigenous peoples was a group of "pygmies" from the African Congo. These men were depicted as a "missing link" between humans and apes and as evidence of "Darwin's theory." Promoting the display, *The St. Louis Republic* reported, "It is believed that the pygmies, who are said to represent the lowest form of human development, are next removed from the Simian family."[30]

Two years later, one of the Congolese men put on display in St. Louis was publicly displayed at the Bronx Zoo in New York City.[31] His name was Ota Benga. This time he was presented in a cage with an orangutan. He also appeared in photographs with a chimpanzee. White and black clergy attacked the display as degrading. Black minister James Gordon declared, "The Darwinian theory is absolutely opposed to Christianity... Neither the Negro nor the white man is related to the monkey, and such an exhibition only degrades a human being's manhood."[32] He added, "We do not like this exhibition of one of our race with the monkeys... We think we are worthy of being considered human beings, with souls."[33] *The New York Times* pooh-poohed the concerns and defended the display: "Whether they [African pygmies] are... really closer to the anthropoid apes than the other African savages, or whether they are viewed as the degenerate descendants of ordinary negroes, they are of equal interest to the student of ethnology, and can be studied with profit."[34]

In 1913, a great-grandson of American Founder John Adams publicly embraced scientific racism. In an address delivered to the faculty and students at the University of South Carolina, Charles Francis Adams Jr. reflected on his service on behalf of the North in the Civil War. Although he still affirmed that slavery in America prior to 1865 had been neither "desirable" nor "justifiable," he went on to say that he and his fellow abolitionists had been "thoroughly wrong" in their belief in human equality:

> In utter disregard of fundamental, scientific facts, we theoretically believed that all men—no matter what might be the color of their skin, or the texture of their hair—were, if placed under exactly similar conditions, in essentials the same. In other words, we indulged in the curious and, as is now admitted, utterly erroneous theory that the African was, so to speak, an Anglo-Saxon… In other words, though carved in ebony, he also was in the image of God.[35]

In short, science had proven that all men had *not* been created equal, and public policy needed to be in accord with that fact. Notice, too, that Adams's language explicitly challenges the biblical teaching of the Imago Dei. That is, he is plainly stating that Darwinism overturns the view that all humans are made in the image of God. (More on this below.)

Adams's speech was later published by the US Senate, apparently on behalf of Democratic Senator Benjamin Tillman from South Carolina.[36] A radical white supremacist, Tillman must have found Adams's talk encouraging. Tillman had previously boasted on the Senate floor that he and others successfully disenfranchised blacks after the Civil War through intimidation, killings, and fraud.[37] Tillman justified his actions by drawing on the standard tropes of evolutionary racism: "We had decided to take the government away from men so debased as were the negroes—I will not say baboons; I never have called them baboons; I believe they are men, but some of them are so near akin to the monkey that scientists are yet looking for the missing link."

Figure 4.2. Proponents of scientific racism. *Each row, left to right, starting at the top:* Charles Darwin, William McGee, Charles Davenport, Edward East, Charles Francis Adams Jr., Benjamin Tillman.

In the years that followed, explicitly Darwinian justifications for racism were offered by some of America's leading scientists. Arguing that "wherever the negro has been placed he has... failed miserably and utterly by the white man's standards," Harvard biologist Edward East said that such a record lent credence to the conclusion of British scientist Karl Pearson that "the negro lies nearer to the common stem" of man's evolutionary tree "than the European."[38] Leading American geneticist Charles Davenport contended that the reason "a smaller proportion" of blacks than whites exhibited "self control," a "special regard for property rights," and an "appreciation of cause and effect" was that "the Negro from Africa... had not evolved in the direction of these traits."[39] Davenport further implied that blacks brought to America on slave ships had been fitted by nature for slavery. "Scores of thousands of black men from the interior of Africa... had been kidnapped by the more enterprising natives that lived along the coast. These negroes represented some of the mentally feeblest races of the globe, with an inborn docility and fidelity which made them good slaves."[40]

To substantiate their claims of negro mental inferiority, Davenport, East, and others cited the results of Army intelligence tests of recruits during World War I.[41] After those tests were discredited, Davenport trumpeted new research in Jamaica purporting to show that "in tests involving some organization, foresight and planning... the negroes seem to be inferior to the whites."[42]

By the 1920s, sweeping new immigration restrictions were imposed in America in cooperation with Darwinian biologists who decided that certain races and people groups were lower on the evolutionary scale and thus needed to be kept out.[43] Blacks were not the only biologically inferior race according to Darwinian scientists. Asians, Native Americans, and whites from southern and eastern Europe were also denigrated.

Since the Civil Rights movement, most American scientists have abandoned Darwinian racism. There are exceptions. In 2007, Nobel-Prize winning biologist James Watson, the co-discoverer of the structure of DNA, sparked an uproar by suggesting that African blacks are biologically inferior to European whites. Watson further suggested that human evolution was the explanation for this biological inferiority.[44] In his words, "There is no firm reason to anticipate that the intellectual capacities of peoples geographically separated in their evolution should prove to have evolved identically." Watson later reaffirmed his views in an interview in 2018.[45]

Outside the scientific community, white supremacists in the so-called "alt-right" have tried to revive Darwinian arguments for racism in recent years. An article in one of the prominent alt-right journals argues, "Darwinism offers a compelling and rational justification for Whites to act on behalf of their ancestors and progeny, and feel a shared sense of destiny with their extended kin group."[46] In a 2017 study, more than four hundred self-identified members of the alt-right revealed that they view blacks, Mexicans, and other racial and ethnic groups as less evolved and closer to humans' ape-like ancestors than to whites.[47] Atheist monarchist Curtis Yarvin has gone so far as to assert that Confederate Alexander Stephens and Charles Francis Adams Jr. were both "right about the facts of the matter" in their racist proclamations.[48]

Worse, renewed evolutionary racism has done more than fuel hateful racist talk; it also has motivated racist acts of violence. In 2009, a white man drove to the Holocaust Museum in Washington, DC, where he fatally shot an African-American security guard. The shooter had previously published a document arguing that "cross-breeding Whites with species lower on the evolutionary scale diminishes the White gene-pool while increasing the number of… mongrels."[49] In 2022, a teenage white male shooter murdered ten blacks at a supermarket in Buffalo, New York. In a manifesto written before the shooting, the killer argued that blacks "are a different subspecies of human" because "Whites and Blacks are separated by tens of thousands of years of evolution, and our genetic material is obviously very different."[50]

As poisonous as Darwinian racism has been in American history and culture, in some ways it was not Darwinism's worst assault on the Declaration's view of the human person. Without question, the

Darwinian claim that some human groups were biologically inferior to others was awful. But Darwinism went even further. It ultimately degraded the status of *every* human being, regardless of race.

The Denial of Human Exceptionalism

The Declaration of Independence's pronouncement that "all men are created equal" assumed that human beings are exceptional among living creatures. Humans as a class share capabilities that make them equally human and that differentiate them from dogs or fishes or fleas. In biblical terms, all humans are equal in reflecting the "image of God" and have eternal souls. In more secular terms, humans possess reason. They have the gift of free will to make choices, which makes them morally responsible for their actions. They create art, music, stories, and inventions. They worship God.

Darwin's theory offered a sharply divergent vision of humanity that blurred the distinction between humans and other animals.

In his book *The Descent of Man*, Darwin wanted to show "that there is no fundamental difference between man and the higher mammals in their mental faculties."[51] The human capacity for reason was not unique, because "animals may constantly be seen to pause, deliberate, and resolve."[52] The human capacity for progressive improvement was not unique, because animals could learn to avoid traps.[53] The human use of tools was not unique because "a chimpanzee in a state of nature cracks a native fruit somewhat like a walnut, with a stone."[54] Even language was nothing special, because it developed from "the imitation and modification, aided by signs and gestures, of various natural sounds, the voices of other animals, and man's own instinctive cries."[55] Thought itself was simply a material product of the body for both humans and animals. "Brain makes thought," Darwin wrote in his private notebooks,[56] and in animals he thought we could see thought "produced as soon as brain developed… no soul superadded," so that "thought… seems as much function of organ, as bile of liver."[57]

Darwin also questioned whether human beings were morally responsible for their actions. In *The Descent of Man*, he explained human behavior as largely the function of pre-determined—and often anti-social—instincts. What did this mean in practice? "At the moment of action," wrote Darwin, "man will no doubt be apt to follow the stronger impulse; and though this may occasionally prompt him to the noblest deeds, it will far more commonly lead him to gratify his own desires at the expense of other men."[58]

Darwin tried to soften the implications of his view by going on to claim that men will learn to regret their impulsive actions and eventually this regret will create in them a conscience. However, Darwin did not convincingly explain why the conscience would trump the instincts that he had earlier depicted as so overwhelming. Even if conscience is able to counteract the antisocial instincts in some men, presumably those who act antisocially are only following their own strongest instincts. If this be the case, how responsible are those who act against society? Not very, suggested Darwin in his unpublished notebooks, where he wrote that "the general delusion about free will [is] obvious," and that one ought to punish criminals "solely to *deter* others"—not because they did something blameworthy.[59] "This view should teach one profound humility," wrote Darwin, "one deserves no credit for anything... nor ought one to blame others." Darwin denied that such a fatalistic view would harm society, believing that ordinary people would never be "*fully* convinced of its truth," and the enlightened few who did embrace it could be trusted.[60]

Even when it comes to worshiping God, humans do not reflect traits substantially different from what we find among other animals, according to Darwin. He was willing to admit that there was an "almost universal" belief in some sort of spiritual world among primitive peoples, but he placed such beliefs on the level of a dog who barks and growls upon seeing an open parasol moved by the wind. Just as the dog mistakenly believes that some intelligent agent moved the parasol, primitive peoples surmised that unseen beings were behind all manner of natural phenomena.[61]

Darwin's theory undermined the Founders' view of humans as uniquely rational and responsible beings, tutoring people to instead believe that humans ultimately were just another animal. Darwin himself recognized that his theory diminished the case for human uniqueness, writing in one of his notebooks that "it is absurd to talk of one animal being higher than another."[62] He also complained that "people often talk of the wonderful event of intellectual Man appearing" when, in fact, "the appearance of insects with other senses is more wonderful."[63]

When in the 1920s Harvard biologist Edward East attacked as unscientific the idea that "man is created in the image of God,"[64] he was merely following in the footsteps of Darwin—as are Darwinian biologists today who relish emphasizing that humans are just another animal. Biologist Charles Zuker says humans "are nothing but a big fly."[65] Geneticist Glen Evans asserts that "the worm represents a very simple human." A science journalist comments that "there isn't much difference between mice and men."[66] And the late Morris Goodman of Wayne State University argued that humans are "only slightly remodeled chimpanzee-like apes."[67]

Darwinian social theorists across the political spectrum make similar claims. John Derbyshire, formerly a writer with the conservative magazine *National Review*, argues approvingly that "the broad outlook on human nature implied by Darwinian ideas contradicts the notion of *human exceptionalism*... To modern biologists, informed by Darwin, we are merely another branch on Nature's tree."[68] Princeton University bioethicist Peter Singer, a political progressive and author of *A Darwinian Left*, agrees. In Singer's words, Darwin "showed... that we are simply animals. Humans had imagined we were a separate part of Creation, that there was some magical line between Us and Them. Darwin's theory undermined the foundations of that entire Western way of thinking about the place of our species in the universe."[69]

The diminishment of human free will and moral responsibility is likewise rampant among contemporary purveyors of Darwinism. "Naturalistic evolution has clear consequences that Charles Darwin understood perfectly," wrote the late William Provine, Professor of History of Biology at Cornell University. One of those consequences, according to Provine, was the idea that "human free will is nonexistent... Free will is a disastrous and mean social myth."[70]

Evolutionary psychology booster Robert Wright made the same argument four years earlier in his bestselling *The Moral Animal*: "Free will is an illusion, brought to us by evolution"[71] and "understanding the often unconscious nature of genetic control is the first step toward understanding that—in many realms, not just sex—we're all puppets."[72] Wright does add that "our best hope for even partial liberation is to try to decipher the logic of the puppeteer."[73] But if "free will is an illusion," precisely how can we liberate ourselves from "the puppeteer"? And if human beings truly are the "puppets" of their genes, puppets whose "emotions are just evolution's executioners"[74] (again quoting Wright), in what sense can people be either blamable or laudable for their behavior?

Darwin's Denial of Human Exceptionalism: Its Far-Reaching Impact in America

Crime and Punishment

By the end of the nineteenth century, American intellectuals were talking with excitement about the "new school of criminal anthropology" that sought to use modern science to identify the causes of crime. Leading the way was Italian criminologist Cesare Lombroso (1835–1909), whose book *Criminal Man* (1876) remains a landmark work in the field of criminology. Lombroso and his disciples contended that criminal behavior could be explained largely as a throwback to earlier stages of Darwinian evolution.[75] As William Noyes, one of Lombroso's American disciples, explained, "in the process of evolution, crime has been one of the necessary accompaniments of the struggle for existence."[76] While crime no longer served a necessary survival function in civilized societies, many modern criminals could be considered atavists—reappearances of characteristics from earlier stages of evolutionary development. According to Lombroso, such atavists were "born criminals," exhibiting from birth the physical as well as behavioral characteristics of savages.[77]

Following Darwin and in contrast to the high view of moral responsibility held by the American Founders, Lombroso and his followers repudiated the idea that "crime involved... moral guilt." Italian jurist Enrico Ferri (1856–1929), one of Lombroso's most celebrated disciples, argued that it was no longer reasonable to believe that human beings could make choices outside the normal chain of material cause and effect, given the advent of modern science, particularly the work of Charles Darwin. Portraying the controversy over Darwin's ideas as nothing less than a battle between the forces of enlightenment and "the lovers of darkness," Ferri applauded Darwin for showing "that man is not the king of creation, but merely the last link of the zoological chain, that nature is endowed with eternal energies by which animal and plant life... are transformed from the invisible microbe to the highest form, man." Ferri looked forward to the day when punishment and vengeance would be abandoned, and crime would be regarded as a "disease" to be treated.[78]

Darwinism was not the only form of scientific materialism to undermine the idea of human responsibility for crime, but it helped lead the way, and it continues to be invoked. In our own day, celebrated psychologist Steven Pinker has argued for more lenient treatment of mothers who commit infanticide, because he thinks they evolved to kill their children. "The emotional circuitry of mothers has evolved" to encourage such behavior under certain circumstances, "so the baby killers turn out to be not moral monsters but nice, normal (and sometimes religious) young women."[79]

Life and Death

Scientists and political activists alike appeal to Darwinian theory to justify abortion by claiming that babies in the womb are not fully human.[80] Invoking an idea known as embryonic recapitulation, these proponents of abortion argue that human infants replay the history of evolution as they develop in the womb. They go through a fish stage, a lower mammal stage, and more before finally reaching the state of a human being. Thus, if someone aborts an infant while she is still in the fish stage, it is no more immoral than killing a fish.

Embryonic recapitulation is junk science and has been discredited even among evolutionary biologists for decades.[81] That has not stopped this argument from being invoked repeatedly as a justification for abortion in public policy debates. In 1981, for example, University of Michigan geneticist James Neel testified to the US Congress that "the early embryo appears to pass through some of the stages in the evolutionary history of our species. The scientific dictum is: 'Ontogeny recapitulates phylogeny,' which translates into: during embryological development we repeat in abbreviated form many aspects of our evolutionary past."[82] Neel told lawmakers that because of "these facts," he found "it most difficult to state, as a scientist, just when in early fetal development human personhood begins, just as I would find it impossible to say exactly when in evolution we passed over the threshold that divides us from the other living creatures." Neel was a member of the National Academy of Sciences and one of America's top geneticists.

The recapitulation argument for abortion has continued to resurface. In 1990, celebrated astronomer Carl Sagan and his wife Ann Druyan published a defense of abortion that relied heavily on the idea of recapitulation.[83] In 2007, the late journalist Christopher Hitchens similarly defended abortion by claiming that "in utero we see a microcosm of nature and evolution itself... we begin as tiny forms that are amphibian."[84]

Darwinism has bled into debates over infanticide as well. University of Chicago evolutionary biologist Jerry Coyne has argued for legalizing infanticide for babies with biological defects. "After all, we euthanize our dogs and cats when to prolong their lives would be torture," he wrote, "so why not extend that to humans?"[85]

Coyne recognizes that the reason we do not do so is because of a view of human beings that Darwinism has yet to completely overcome: "The reason we don't allow euthanasia of newborns is because humans are seen as special, and I think this comes from religion—in particular, the view that humans, unlike animals, are endowed with a soul... When religion vanishes, as it will, so will much of the opposition to both adult and newborn euthanasia."

Man and Nature

A similarly Darwinian devaluation of human life can be found among radical environmentalists.[86] University of Texas evolutionary zoologist

Eric Pianka argued that "humans are no better than bacteria,"[87] and "other things on this earth have been here longer than us… and they have a right to this planet too—that includes wasps that sting you, ants that bite you, scorpions and rattlesnakes."[88] Pianka went on to criticize humans for "sucking everything we can out of mother Earth and turning it into fat human bio-mass."[89] Pianka urged the reduction of the Earth's human population by up to 90 percent and called on the government to confiscate all the earnings of any couple who has more than two children. "You should have to pay more when you have your first kid—you pay more taxes," he insists. "When you have your second kid you pay a lot more taxes, and when you have your third kid you don't get anything back, they take it all."[90]

Underlying the radical environmentalists' hatred for humans is the Darwinian rejection of human uniqueness. Christopher Manes, one of the early leaders of the environmentalist group Earth First!, explains: "Darwin invited humanity to face the fact that the observation of nature has revealed not one scrap of evidence that humankind is superior or special, or even particularly more interesting than, say, lichen."[91]

This kind of Darwinian misanthropy motivated eco-terrorist James Lee, who in 2010 took staff of the Discovery Channel hostage. Lee called on the Discovery Channel to "Talk about Evolution. Talk about Malthus and Darwin until it sinks into the stupid people's brains until they get it!"[92] Lee's stated goal was to save "what's left of the non-human Wildlife by decreasing the Human population. That means stopping the human race from breeding any more disgusting human babies!"

Life After Death

The Darwinian account of humans also encouraged the rejection of an immaterial human soul that transcends death. In the words of nineteenth-century German physiologist Emil Du Bois-Reymond, "The evolution theory in connection with the doctrine of natural selection forces upon [humankind]… the idea that the soul has arisen as the gradual result of certain material combinations."[93] Noted evolutionist

Stephen Jay Gould expressed the same view, arguing that according to Darwin's theory "matter is the ground of all existence: mind, spirit, and God as well, are just words that express the wondrous results of neuronal complexity."[94]

The Denial of a Natural Moral Law

The Declaration of Independence appealed to the authority of the "laws of Nature and Nature's God." As discussed in Chapter 2, the Founders were referring to the idea that there are laws of morality that are obligatory across time and place and can be known both through the Bible and conscience. Darwinism undermined this view as well.

According to Darwin, specific moral precepts developed because under certain environmental conditions they promoted survival.[95] Once those conditions for survival change, however, so too do the dictates of morality. That is why we find in nature both the maternal instinct and infanticide, both honoring one's parents and killing them when they become feeble. Natural selection "chooses" whatever behavioral traits best promote survival under the existing circumstances.

A Darwinian understanding of morality makes it very difficult to condemn as evil any human behavior that has persisted, because every trait that continues to exist even among a subpopulation has an equal right to claim nature's sanction—presumably even antisocial behaviors such as fraud, pedophilia, and rape because they too apparently were favored at some point by natural selection. Of course, one could still justly condemn such behaviors if there existed a permanent moral standard independent of natural selection. But the existence of such a standard is precisely what orthodox Darwinism denies.

For the most part, Darwin himself did not press his relativistic analysis of morality to its logical conclusion, but he laid the groundwork for others who came after him, and his ideas helped reshape how people think about morality. For example, 44 percent of Americans now believe that "what is right and wrong evolves over time based on the survival needs of a society."[96] Robert Wright is correct to observe that the "Darwinian paradigm" has the effect of "nourishing a certain moral relativism—if not, indeed, an outright cynicism about moral codes in general."[97]

Nowhere has the Darwinian view of ethics had a severer impact than in family life and human sexuality. The thinker most responsible for the breakdown of traditional sexual ethics in Western culture was Harvard-trained evolutionary zoologist Alfred Kinsey. Adopting a thoroughly Darwinian approach to sexual morality, Kinsey argued that any sexual practice that could be found somewhere among mammals could be regarded as "normal mammalian behavior" and be regarded as unobjectionable.[98]

Today, many evolutionary psychologists have gone beyond mere sexual relativism and are affirmatively arguing against monogamy. They claim that we were bred by Darwinian evolution to have multiple sex partners, which means we are programmed for promiscuity and infidelity. In their view, the very idea of faithful monogamous marriage contradicts our biology and must therefore be abandoned.

One prominent evolutionary psychologist to advocate this view is Christopher Ryan, co-author of the *New York Times* bestseller, *Sex at Dawn*. In the words of Ryan, "Marriage in the West isn't doing very well because it's in direct confrontation with the evolved reality of our species."[99] Ryan says he wants to save marriage by making it consistent with Darwinian biology. For him, that means redefining marriage to include multiple partners at the same time.

The end result for those who try to embrace a consistent Darwinian worldview isn't just relativism. It is a rejection of all objective standards whatsoever.

The philosopher Friedrich Nietzsche observed that Darwin's theory was "true but deadly."[100] Nietzsche accepted as true Darwin's account that there is no radical difference between man and beast and that all species and ideas (including moral ideas) are forever in flux. But he understood that this denial of unchanging morality and unchanging biological categories raised the danger of nihilism—complete meaninglessness because nothing can be regarded as really true. Nietzsche's solution was to call for a "superman" who would create a moral code and impose it on society.[101] Our culture has democratized Nietzsche. Now everyone is their own superman and everyone is encouraged to create his or her own reality, including sexual identity.

This can be seen in the current debate over transgenderism. In the pre-Darwinian view, male and female were objective and permanent categories created by God for our good. If you feel uncomfortable as a man or a woman, you can be assured that your biological sex reflects something greater than your feelings and that you should embrace it. But in the Darwinian view, male and female are simply categories produced by an accidental process in natural history that could have produced other outcomes. There is nothing permanent or sacrosanct about two biological sexes. Moreover, natural selection apparently somehow led to your feelings of being "in the wrong body," so you should feel free to revolt against your body. The only question is whether you have the technical power to change yourself into something else.

Needless to say, this new view of morality is toxic to the Founders' understanding of liberty. By the Founders' lights, liberty involved acting within the guardrails of the moral law. But if there is no moral law, liberty devolves into simple libertinism, fueling cultural anarchy.

The Denial of Limited Government

The great majority of Americans today believe in expansive government. Nearly 80 percent say that "the purposes of government should change over time based on the evolving needs of society."[102] Nearly 70 percent believe the government should guarantee "education, medical care, and an adequate income for everyone." New York City mayor Zohran Mamdani expressed the view of a growing number of Americans when upon his election he declared, "We will prove that there is no problem too large for government to solve, and no concern too small for it to care about."[103]

By contrast, the Declaration of Independence articulates the unchanging purpose of government as securing people's unalienable rights to life, liberty, and the pursuit of happiness. This basically means establishing a society where people can pursue their own goals based on their own efforts within the confines of the laws of Nature and Nature's God. In such a society, people are free to produce goods and services, raise crops and livestock, create art and music, pursue scientific discovery, invent new devices, debate ideas, raise their families, and worship God according to the dictates of their own consciences.

The Founders did not think that the purposes of government included providing everyone with the same income, guaranteeing everyone a healthy body, protecting people from the vicissitudes of daily life, or securing for them eternal salvation. The Declaration called for *limited* government, and the Founders established one in the Constitution of 1787.

Over half a century later, writer Henry David Thoreau pithily encapsulated the American philosophy of limited government thus: "I heartily accept the motto—'That government is best which governs least'; and I should like to see it acted up to more rapidly and systematically."[104] Thoreau was trying to point out that many achievements in society are ultimately due to the efforts of free individuals, not government: "This government never of itself furthered any enterprise, but by the alacrity with which it got out of the way. *It* does not keep the country free. *It* does not settle the West. *It* does not educate. The character inherent in the American people has done all that has been accomplished; and it would have done somewhat more, if the government had not sometimes got in its way."[105]

Even in the time of Thoreau, some might have objected to his claims by pointing out that the government *does* play a role in the things he listed. Yet if we reflect upon matters more, I think we can see that Thoreau has a point. Government officials may decide to repel an invasion, but without patriotic citizens to follow their call to arms, the nation is doomed. The government may fund schools and hire teachers, but students are the ones who ultimately have to do the hard work in order to learn. And while government policies certainly encouraged the settlement of the West, without the dreams, tenacity, and sacrifices of the pioneers, nothing would have been settled. Thoreau's emphasis on the primacy of free individuals over the government echoed the views of the Founders.

However, by the end of the century, a radically new conception of government and political society had taken hold in America, one at odds with the ideas of the Founders.

Columbia University professor John Burgess helped develop the discipline of political science in the United States. He exemplified the new vision of government and politics. In 1890, he defined "the universal human purpose of the state" as "the perfection of humanity; the civilization of the world; the perfect development of the human reason, and its attainment to universal command over individualism; the apotheosis of man."[106] The word "apotheosis" literally means to change someone into a god.[107] So, according to Burgess, the end of the state is to turn man into a god. For Burgess, *state* meant more than just government, but the distinction was soon lost by others.

The new view of politics repudiated the natural rights philosophy of the Founders. University of Chicago political scientist Charles Merriam (1874–1953) was especially influential. In 1920 he noted that among recent thinkers "the idea that men possess inherent and inalienable rights of a political or quasi-political character which are independent of the state, has been generally given up."[108] The result has been "a decided tendency away from many doctrines that were held by the men of 1776."[109] In particular, "Revolutionary doctrines" such as "natural rights" and "the idea that the function of the government is limited to the protection of person and property... none of these finds wide acceptance among the [new] leaders in the development of political science."

At the time of the Founders, "nature" meant the inherent order of things ordained by God and reason. It represented a permanent standard of right across time and place. But for the new political scientists, "nature" was simply the physical natural world, and the law of nature applicable to humans was Darwin's law of the jungle. In the words of historian Carl Becker in 1922, "When so much the greater part of the universe showed itself amenable to the reign of a purely material natural law, it was difficult to suppose that man (a creature in many respects astonishingly like the higher forms of apes) could have been permitted to live under a special dispensation. It was much simpler to assume one origin for all life and one law for all growth."[110] That meant we should think of humanity's history "as only a more subtly negotiated struggle for existence and survival." Or as political scientist Westel Willoughby at Johns Hopkins University put it in 1896, the laws of nature were simply "the natural instincts of all living beings, men and brutes alike, to maintain their own existences, and to satisfy the desires that their own natures give rise to. Under such a regime... an unmitigated and pitiless struggle for existence must prevail."[111]

In this new view of politics, liberty was no longer regarded as "a natural right which belongs to every human being without regard to the state or society under which he lives."[112] Instead, liberty is a privilege bestowed by the state and "is dependent upon the degree of civilization reached by the given people." Moreover, "the inseparable connection between political liberty and political capacity is strongly emphasized." There was a racist tinge to the new view of malleable rights. According to Merriam, the Teutonic (white European) race had the most capacity for liberty. Hence, in nations with multiple nationalities, wrote Merriam, "the Teutonic element should never surrender the balance of power to the others."[113] The "Teutonic race can never regard the exercise of political power as a right of man, but it must always be their policy to condition the exercise of political rights on the possession of political capacity."

On the view of such thinkers, because there are no natural or God-given rights that governments must always respect, the powers of government are no longer inherently limited. "The determination of just what powers shall be assumed by the State, is solely one of expediency... This is practically the rule followed by all modern civilized States."[114] In sum, the powers and scope of government were no longer static. They evolved according to what a people needed in order to survive and flourish.

The ultimate roots of this progressive idea of political evolution were likely supplied by Georg Wilhelm Friedrich Hegel and the political science of the German administrative state.[115] But Darwin was honored for showing that the truths preached by the political philosophers had been substantiated by biological science.

One of the most articulate spokesmen for the new view was a political scientist from New Jersey, who argued that "in our own day, whenever we discuss the structure or development of anything... we consciously or unconsciously follow Mr. Darwin."[116] The political scientist was Woodrow Wilson, then president of Princeton, soon to be governor of New Jersey and eventually president of the United States. During the presidential election campaign of 1912, Wilson explicitly invoked Darwin to justify an evolutionary understanding of the US Constitution that would allow the federal government to dramatically expand its powers over the economy.

On Wilson's view, the problem with the original Constitution was that it betrayed the Founders' "Newtonian" view that government was built on unchanging laws like "the law of gravitation."[117] In truth, however, government "falls, not under the theory of the universe, but under the theory of organic life. It is accountable to Darwin, not to Newton. It is modified by its environment, necessitated by its tasks, shaped to its functions by the sheer pressure of life."[118] Hence, "living political constitutions must be Darwinian in structure and in practice. Society is a living organism and must obey the laws of life... it must develop." According to Wilson, "All that progressives ask or desire is permission—in an era when 'development,' 'evolution,' is the scientific word—to interpret the Constitution according to the Darwinian principle."[119] The doctrine of the evolving Constitution articulated by Wilson and other progressives opened the door to much greater regulation of business and the economy, eventually paving the way for the New Deal, the Great Society, and the nearly unlimited government of our own era.

There was an additional way Darwinism eroded the Founders' system of limited government. The right to liberty and the pursuit of happiness encompassed the right to acquire property and the right to benefit from the fruits of one's labor and industry. A key argument against the morality of slavery was the injustice of depriving a man of the fruits of his labor. In classical economics, business activity was not a zero-sum game. All parties benefited from uncoerced and honest economic transactions. But in the late nineteenth and early twentieth

Figure 4.3. Proponents of the new "scientific" theory of politics. *Each row, left to right, starting at the top:* John Burgess, Charles Merriam, Westel Willoughby, Woodrow Wilson, Carl Becker.

centuries, various left-wing reformers tried to discredit this capitalist system by claiming it was nothing more than brutish Darwinian "survival of the fittest" applied to the world of business. According to historian Robert Bannister, "New Liberals and socialists asserted in almost a single voice that opponents of state activity wedded Darwinism to classical economics and thus traded illicitly on the prestige of the new biology."[120] As a result, the primary use of the epithet "Social Darwinism" was not to justify capitalism, but to stigmatize it in order to undermine its legitimacy and generate support for expanded government control over the economy. Darwinism became one of the most potent rhetorical weapons in the arsenal of those who wanted to attack free enterprise.[121]

The Denial of Consent of the Governed

Because all men are created equal, governments derive "their just powers from the consent of the governed" according to the Declaration of Independence. But in the new age of scientism, this proposition came under sustained attack as well. Science came to be viewed as the ultimate source of knowledge and wisdom about the world, so by extension it was natural to conclude that scientists alone should hold the keys to all true knowledge, including the true knowledge of proper governance. It was but a small step from here to conclude that scientists rather than ordinary voters or their elected representatives should be the ones to rule.

Accordingly, American sociologist Lester Frank Ward in the 1890s called for "the scientific control of the social forces by the collective mind of society for its advantage."[122] This required a complete transformation of government "into a central academy of social science, which shall stand in the same relation to the control of men in which a polytechnic institute stands to the control of nature."[123]

Speaking at a conference in New York in 1921, Alleyne Ireland made clear what these new ideas meant for America's original form of government established by the Constitution and the Declaration of Independence. Ireland declared that current conditions had rendered America's original system of government "utterly unsuitable."

America's Founders believed that "governments derive their just powers from the consent of the governed," and they set up arrangements "designed with a view to making abuse of power difficult." But in an age when government must increasingly provide a wide range of social services, reasoned Ireland, society could no longer afford to rely on government by non-experts. Instead, it was "imperative... that the omnipresent activity of government should be guided by the light of scientific knowledge and conducted through the instrumentality of a scientific method."[124]

The call for scientocracy was fueled by utopian rhetoric from those who claimed to speak for science. Around the turn of the twentieth century, scientists began issuing increasingly lofty claims about how science's understanding of the material world could be used to solve all the problems of human society. The same scientific advances that produced inventions like the steam engine and medical breakthroughs like the germ theory of disease were also supposed to supply the basis for eliminating a host of social ills ranging from poverty to crime to unproductive workers.

Writing in the journal *Science* in 1903, J. McKeen Cattell, president of the American Society of Naturalists, argued that science's previous achievements in helping man to subjugate the natural world were just a foretaste of the future power science would bestow on man to control human nature. "The nineteenth century witnessed an extraordinary increase in our knowledge of the material world and in our power to make it subservient to our ends," he wrote. "The twentieth century will probably witness a corresponding increase in our knowledge of human nature and in our power to use it for our welfare."[125]

Charles Eliot, president of the American Association for the Advancement of Science, similarly predicted that "biological science" would open the door to the "prevention as well as cure" of the "bodily defects" that caused such antisocial behaviors as murder, robbery, forgery, and prostitution. "These are all biological problems," he declared, "and the progress of biological inquiry during the past fifty years is sufficient to afford the means of solving" them.[126]

The new scientific utopians essentially rejected another core belief of the Founders: human imperfectibility. As was discussed in the previous chapters, the Founders thought that humans were equal not only in certain positive attributes, but also in a negative one. They were all corruptible. But according to the scientific utopians, human nature was not fixed; it could be remade through the methods of modern science. Men may not be angels now, but under the right biological and environmental conditioning, they might become angelic. Scientific breeding, conditioning, and medical treatment could usher in a new age only dreamt of by previous reformers. In short, scientific materialism undermined the very premises of American political realism.

The example *par excellence* of this new fusion of science, utopianism, and raw political power was something known as eugenics. Described by its proponents as the self-direction of human evolution, eugenics was enacted by politicians, but it was implemented at the behest of scientists who claimed that their expertise trumped objections from ordinary people, especially Catholics and Christian fundamentalists.

The inspiration for eugenics sprang directly from Darwin's theory. In Darwin's view, the key reason humans developed their outstanding capabilities was not because they were designed that way by a Creator, but because natural selection ruthlessly weeded out the unfit. The problem according to eugenicists was that in the name of humanitarianism, civilized societies were now doing their best to care for those whom nature would have killed off. The eugenicists were convinced that this would lead to disaster.

In *The Descent of Man,* Darwin criticized modern society for methodically undermining natural selection's "process of elimination" by offering asylums for the mentally ill, homes for the handicapped, hospitals for the sick, and welfare programs for the poor.[127] Darwin even warned about the dangers of vaccinating people against smallpox, which he thought "preserved thousands, who from a weak constitution would formerly have succumbed." Darwin's stark conclusion: "Thus the weak members of civilised societies propagate their kind. No one who has attended to the breeding of domestic animals will doubt that this must be highly injurious to the race of man… hardly any one is so ignorant as to allow his worst animals to breed."

A kindly man, Darwin was torn by the implications of his theory, and he thought human sympathy would not allow people to follow his theory to its logical conclusion. Likewise, many of his followers believed it would be too cruel for humans to go back to the law of the jungle. They wanted to develop a kinder way to mimic natural selection through modern science. That was the goal of eugenics.

Charles Darwin's cousin, Francis Galton, is generally recognized as the official founder of eugenics, and he actually coined the term (adapted from a Greek root word meaning "good in birth"[128]). "Positive eugenics" focused on encouraging those deemed the most fit to reproduce more, while "negative eugenics" focused on curtailing reproduction by those deemed "unfit," including mental defectives and criminals. Eugenics became the consensus view of the scientific community for decades, and it was promoted by leading scientists around the world. In America, eugenics supporters included biologists at Harvard, Princeton, Yale, Columbia, Stanford, and the National Academy of Scientists.[129] In retrospect, most scientists now view eugenics as little more than junk science, and there is general recognition that eugenicists' judgments about who were "unfit" were notoriously subjective and often tinged by racial prejudice. Eugenicists also presented the public with a false set of choices about social policy.[130] Nevertheless, it's hard to overstate how much support the eugenics crusade drew from mainstream science in general and Darwinian biology in particular.

Today the Darwinian roots of eugenics tend to be downplayed, but the Darwinian rationale for eugenics was explicit in the writings of eugenicists themselves. For example, Harvard geneticist Edward East insisted that "eugenic tenets are strict corollaries" of "the theory of organic evolution."[131] Princeton biologist Edwin Conklin similarly advocated for eugenics as a way to undo modern society's violation of "natural selection, the great law of evolution and progress."[132]

Eugenics was sold with heaping dollops of scientific utopianism. "The Garden of Eden is not in the past, it is in the future!" promised eugenicist Albert Wiggam.[133] US Secretary of Agriculture James "Tama Jim" Wilson in 1913 acknowledged that the wholesale replacement of "inferior" human stocks with "the best part of the human race... at first seems like an Utopian vision," but he quickly added, "Why should it not come? Must science stop in its beneficence with the plant and the animal? Is not man, after all, the architect of his own racial destiny?"[134]

Figure 4.4. Eugenics exhibition at the American Museum of Natural History in 1932. Note the busts at the entrance to the exhibit of the two men regarded as the founding fathers of eugenics: Charles Darwin and his cousin Francis Galton.

The impact of eugenics on American public policy and culture was far-ranging, including laws on who could marry, immigration restrictions on races considered lower on the evolutionary scale, and forced sterilization of those considered less fit in Darwinian terms. In America, 60,000 women were sterilized against their will in the name of eugenics.[135]

Elsewhere around the world the impact of Darwinian eugenics was even more horrifying. Germany's eugenics movement sterilized hundreds of thousands of people and murdered 300,000 disabled children and adults, many in gas chambers dressed up as shower stalls. It was during the "eugenic" killings of the handicapped that the Nazis developed some of the methods they used to later murder millions of Jews.[136]

After the general public learned about the atrocities committed in the name of eugenics in Nazi Germany, Darwinian eugenics was widely discredited. But the idea that government policy should be increasingly in the hands of scientific experts has persisted.

In our own day, anyone who has followed debates over climate change or transgenderism, or lived through the COVID pandemic, should be able to discern that we are still living with this final repudiation of the Founders' system of limited government constrained by the consent of the governed.

Figure 5.1. "Woodland Landscape" (1850) by Asher Brown Durand.

5. Back to the Future

Like many Americans in the years after America's Founding, Asher Durand was not born into wealth or privilege. He was never a military hero. He never held public office. He did not grow up in a big city. Most people today probably never heard of him. Yet Asher Durand played an important role in popularizing the Declaration of Independence to his countrymen and in reinforcing the Founders' transcendent view of nature during America's first century.[1]

Durand was born in 1796 into a New Jersey community so small that his son later commented that "the few houses… could scarcely be called a village; there was no blacksmith's shop, no grocery and dry-goods store, no tavern furnishing a lodging-place for wayfarers, or a bar for toper or politician, and no church."[2] Pious inhabitants had to walk to another town to attend worship on Sundays.

Durand's father was descended from French Huguenots, Calvinist Christians "driven by persecution to this country."[3] At age seven, Durand was sent to his community's only formal institution, "the village public school," where he recalled instruction "in reading, writing, and arithmetic, a little geography, and the whole of the Westminster Catechism."[4]

After the enactment of the Declaration of Independence, this tiny community had decided to take a name for itself: "Jefferson Village," in honor of the Declaration's primary drafter.[5] Like many small communities of the era, the families of Jefferson Village strove to be self-sufficient and help each other rather than rely on handouts from the government. Without any political theorist having to tell them, they knew the importance of self-government. "On the promulgation of the Declaration of Independence," Durand's son later reported, "the popular mind was thus well prepared to accept and act in accordance with its telling abstractions."[6]

Durand came from a family of artisans, and at age seventeen he was apprenticed to an engraver.[7] By his twenties, he was working on his own. He was fiercely patriotic. During the War of 1812, he and one of his brothers built retrenchments on Long Island to protect against a feared British landing.[8] At age twenty, in 1817, he was selected as "orator of the day" for the July 4th celebration in the Presbyterian Church of the nearest township.[9] After a patriotic procession including fife and drum (played by two of his brothers), Durand presented his oration. He told his fellow citizens that America was "the last hope of human greatness" and "the last asylum for the rights of man."[10] He also expressed gratitude to God. "When we contemplate the astonishing progress of this Republic, have we not cause to look up to Heaven with eternal gratitude?" he asked. He confidently assured his listeners that "the hand of the Eternal guards [America] from destruction."

Durand's big opportunity came three years later. In 1820, he was commissioned by John Trumbull to create an engraving of Trumbull's iconic painting "The Declaration of Independence," which depicted the presentation of the draft Declaration to the Continental Congress.[11] Trumbull's larger-than-life artwork measures twelve by eighteen feet, and it is still displayed in the US Capitol Rotunda. A Revolutionary War veteran, Trumbull had made his career painting scenes from the Revolution. But his painting about the Declaration of Independence is known today largely because of Durand's superb engraving, which took three years to complete. The engraving made it possible for every American to see the painting for themselves, and it made the painting Trumbull's most popular work.

A quintessential American success story, Durand went on to achieve significant success as an engraver. But his greatest fame was yet to come.

He became one of the most acclaimed landscape painters in America and one of the founders of the Hudson River School of landscape painting. And it was in his capacity as a painter that he tried to communicate one of the key beliefs of the Founders to a new generation.

The Founders believed that the natural world provided evidence for God as Creator. Durand believed the same thing. He spoke of "the great miracle of God's creation"[12] and argued that "the true province of Landscape Art is the representation of the work of God in the visible creation."[13] Indeed, "the Great Designer of these glorious pictures [in nature] has placed them before us as types of the Divine attributes."[14] Durand and his fellow painters sought to convey the truth of God's design and beauty in nature through their art.

But even as they enchanted the public with their paintings, times were changing.

About the same time that Durand shifted to landscape painting, a young man more than ten years his junior was sailing the world to explore the mysteries of the nature. In 1832, while walking in the midst of a Brazilian rainforest, this young man was overwhelmed by wonder and awe. Surely, he thought, "there is more in man than the mere breath of his body."[15]

At the time, the young man could have been a kindred spirit of Durand. His name was Charles Darwin.

Unfortunately, Darwin's sense of the transcendent in nature did not survive. Reflecting near the end of his life on his earlier sense of awe in the rainforest, Darwin reported that now not even "the grandest scenes" in nature would inspire such a reaction.[16] The evidence of exquisite design and purpose he previously saw in nature failed once he had formulated his law of natural selection.[17] Tragically, Darwin also reported that "now for many years I cannot endure to read a line of poetry... I have also almost lost my taste for pictures or music... My mind seems to have become a kind of machine for grinding general laws out of large collections of facts."[18] Darwin's view of nature seems to have left him empty.

Asher Durand never gave up his own appreciation for nature. He passed away peacefully on September 17, 1886.[19] The day marked the ninety-ninth anniversary of the signing of the Constitution. He began his career by popularizing the Declaration of Independence. He died on the anniversary of the document that implemented the Declaration's vision.

By the time Durand passed, Darwin was already dead. But his poisonous ideas were not. They were well on their way to persuading cultural elites to abandon the Founders' transcendent view of both man and nature. As recounted in the previous chapter, the new vision of politics was informed by a materialist brand of science which denied that rights came from God, that the ends of government are unchanging, and that all men are created equal.

But it turns out that the triumph of this outlook, which came to dominate academia and much of the culture, is not the end of the story. In a surprising turnabout, science has found its way back to the truths of the Founders and their view of nature.

I first became aware of this shift thirty years ago.

The Surprising Rebirth of Nature's God

A few weeks before Christmas in 1993, the *Wall Street Journal* published an essay with the provocative title "A Scopes Trial for the '90s."[20] The original Scopes trial in 1925 involved the prosecution of high school teacher John Scopes in Tennessee, charged with teaching students the theory of human evolution, contrary to state law. In pop culture, especially in the stage play and film *Inherit the Wind*, the Scopes trial was depicted as an iconic example of Christian fundamentalists trying to persecute a courageous scientist and censor the advance of scientific knowledge.[21]

The new Scopes mentioned in the *Journal* article was Dean Kenyon, a biology professor at San Francisco State University. A senior researcher with a PhD from Stanford, Kenyon had been removed from teaching an introductory biology class—but not because he had taught evolution. Quite the opposite. He had raised scientific criticisms of Darwin's theory in class and disclosed to students his view that living creatures show evidence of "intelligent design."

At the time, I was on staff with Discovery Institute, a small think tank in Seattle that had just been launched in 1991. Bruce Chapman,

Discovery's president, read the *Journal* article, clipped it, and handed it to me. Both of us were intrigued. Like most people, we were used to hearing that objections to Darwin's theory must be based on religion and that the only people persecuted for their views about evolution were those who defended it. So here was a proverbial man bites dog story: A reputable scientist offered a scientific critique of Darwinism and faced persecution for his views.

Having just spent several years in grad school in California, I found the professor's predicament rather strange. At most California universities, you could believe in almost anything, including the need to overthrow the United States government and replace it with a Communist utopia, and still be tolerated. But questioning Darwin was apparently too much, even for free-thinking Californians.

Bruce noticed that the author of the *Journal* article lived in Washington state. His name was Stephen Meyer. A college professor in his thirties, Meyer had earned his PhD in the history and philosophy of science from the University of Cambridge, and he was teaching philosophy at Whitworth, a liberal arts college in Spokane, Washington. Bruce suggested we reach out to him, and I invited him to Seattle during the next summer to present a lecture in a program I ran for college students for Discovery.

The talk he gave changed the course of my life.

Before meeting Meyer, I already knew that science had been misused in the nineteenth century to advance the worldview of materialism—the idea that everything (including us) could be completely explained as the products of unthinking matter and energy.

Meyer now supplied me with more of the background. Darwin had claimed to explain how complex life could develop through an unguided evolutionary process of natural selection acting on random variations in nature. But Darwin's theory of biological evolution assumed that simple life already existed. Other scientists soon developed theories of chemical evolution purporting to explain how the first life could have arisen as well through an unguided process.

The idea was to show that all of life—including us—could be fully explicated as the products of a blind material process without any need for a Creator. Those who advocated this sweeping claim gained traction because they insisted their view was based on *science.*

In his lecture, Meyer made a startling counter-claim: The scientific materialists were wrong. Instead of proving materialism, the discoveries of science over the past century actually overthrew it.

He explained that the quest to demonstrate the development of life from non-life helped show this. Life is built from non-living chemical molecules known as proteins. But the development of those proteins is dependent on detailed instructions encoded in a chemical compound known as DNA. Without this chemically encoded information, there could be no life.

But where did the information required to build these proteins come from? Scientific materialists hoped they could explain the information as the result of an unguided physical process of chemical interactions plus chance. But the more they investigated, the more it appeared that the information encoded by DNA could not be explained by matter alone. Just as the laws of chemistry cannot explain the information content of the ink on the page of a newspaper, they cannot explain the information content—the instructions—encoded by DNA. These instructions required a mind. The obvious conclusion according to Meyer? The information found at the foundation of life is the product of a cosmic mind.

In other words, the scientific materialists had it precisely backwards. When you reached into the heart of living things, it wasn't unthinking matter all the way down. You found evidence of mind.

I quickly grasped that if what Meyer was saying was true, it would be revolutionary.

By the early twentieth century, much of elite Western culture had embraced the scientific materialism proffered by Darwin and others. In the previous chapter, I discussed the far-ranging consequences of our surrender to scientific materialism. But if Meyer was correct, science itself was now moving away from materialism and toward a non-material cause of reality—an intelligent Creator.

Unfortunately, most people were oblivious to what was happening. Public discussions of science and faith at the time were still mired in the old stereotype that religion was at war with science and that science supported materialism.

In fact, the stereotype was being given new life by a group of articulate scientific atheists who aggressively evangelized for materialism. Chief among them was Oxford University evolutionary biologist Richard Dawkins. His atheistic materialism was founded squarely on Darwin's unguided theory of evolution. As Dawkins famously declared, "Darwin made it possible to be an intellectually fulfilled atheist"[22] and "the universe we observe has precisely the properties we should expect if there is, at bottom, no design, no purpose, no evil and no good, nothing but blind pitiless indifference."[23]

For a time, Dawkins appeared to speak for a growing group of scientific atheists. As they grew in influence and prominence, the group eventually became dubbed the "new atheists." If one trusted the hype, the future was theirs.

Yet if what Meyer told me was true, the Emperor of scientific materialism had no clothes. Despite the bravado of scientific atheists like Dawkins, the accumulating discoveries of science were pointing in the other direction.

Meyer told me about an informal network of a new generation of scientists and scholars who had become convinced that Darwinian materialism was not borne out by the science. Many of them also thought nature was supplying positive evidence of intelligent design by a Creator. But because of the stranglehold of materialism among America's academic elites, they faced an uphill battle in trying to do their research and publish their findings. We became convinced that these scientists and scholars needed a platform to investigate, discuss, and disseminate the scientific findings that ran counter to the claims of Dawkins and his allies. So with the encouragement of Bruce Chapman, Meyer and I co-founded the Center for Science and Culture at Discovery Institute in 1996 with that goal in view.

Three decades later, the landscape has changed dramatically. There is now growing recognition that the onslaught of scientific atheism failed, and members of the cultural elite as well as ordinary people seem open to considering the reality of God. The vibe shift is encapsulated in the title of a recent book: *The Surprising Rebirth of Belief in God.*[24] Part of its subtitle reads: "Why New Atheism Grew Old." As Meyer had predicted in the 1990s, science itself became ground zero for the overthrow of scientific materialism.

In the process, science in our day has come around to re-affirming three truths articulated by the natural theologians and by America's Founders: There is a Creator. All men are created equal. And because of human equality, governments should be based on consent of the governed.

The Case for a Creator

In 2021, Meyer published his book *Return of the God Hypothesis* to widespread acclaim.[25] The book tells the story of how three significant scientific discoveries during the past century have provided powerful evidence for a Creator.

Scientific Discovery #1: The Universe Had a Beginning

From ancient times, various thinkers evaded the need for a Creator by insisting that the universe is eternal and thus had no need of a cause to bring it into existence.

But in the early twentieth century, things changed.

Russian Orthodox physicist Alexander Friedmann, Belgian Catholic priest and physicist Georges Lemaître, American astronomer Edwin Hubble, and other scientists uncovered evidence that the universe did not always exist.[26] This evidence ultimately convinced the scientific community as a whole that our universe was not eternal after all. It began in an initial event that has come to be known as "the Big Bang."[27] Nobel Prize-winning physicist and astronomer Arno Penzias made some of the discoveries that corroborated the idea of a cosmic beginning. Penzias, who was Jewish, told *The New York Times* that "the best data we have are exactly what I would have predicted, had I had nothing to go on but the five books of Moses, the Psalms, the Bible as a whole."[28]

Even some non-religious scientists saw the implications of this discovery. If the universe had a beginning, it needed something to bring it into existence. It required a cause—a Creator. Robert Jastrow was one of America's top astronomers. A professor at Yale and founder of the Goddard Institute at NASA, Jastrow didn't believe in God, but he found it hard to get around what the Big Bang seemed to be telling him.

"So there is a beginning, there is a point in time from which it all started," Jastrow told an interviewer. "And that's a remarkable thing which has a very strong theological flavor to it, and that intrigued me because I am an agnostic, and if there was beginning, a moment of creation in the universe, then there was a creator."[29]

Physicist Brian Miller goes further: "The Big Bang shows that all of time, matter, space and energy, started at a single moment in the past. Therefore, whatever started it has to be outside of time and space."[30] And the cause has to be immaterial, because before the Big Bang, matter didn't exist. In other words, according to Miller, the universe required a cause that is "immaterial, timeless, infinitely powerful, and even personal, because only a personal being can choose to act with purpose."[31] Who does that sound like?

While there have been various speculative scenarios proposed to get around this basic logic, none have gained widespread acceptance.[32]

Scientific Discovery #2: The Universe Is Fine-Tuned for Life

The second discovery is that the laws of physics were exquisitely fine-tuned to enable life to exist. In the words of physicist Freeman Dyson, "The more I examine the universe and study the details of its architecture, the more evidence I find that the universe in some sense must have known that we were coming."[33]

Biologist Michael Denton explains: "There are four fundamental forces in nature according to physicists. These have to be almost exactly as they are to have stable planets, to have galaxies, and to have earths like our planet."[34]

If the gravitational force were weaker, stars or galaxies would not be able to form.[35] If the gravitational force were stronger, the universe itself would collapse. If the strong nuclear force were smaller, the only stable element in the universe would be hydrogen. If the strong nuclear force were greater, there would be no hydrogen. Without hydrogen, there would be no water. Without water, there likely would be no life.

Figure 5.2. Notable scientists who concluded that there is evidence of cosmic purpose in nature. *Clockwise, starting from top left:* Cambridge physicist Fred Hoyle (1915–2001), "A common sense interpretation of the facts suggests that a superintellect has monkeyed with physics, as well as with chemistry and biology." | Nobel laureate physicist Charles Townes (1915–2015), "Intelligent design, as one sees it from a scientific point of view, seems to be quite real." | Nobel laureate physicist Brian Josephson (1940–), "intelligent design is valid science." | National Academy of Sciences physicist Freeman Dyson (1923–2020), "The more I examine the universe… the more evidence I find that the universe in some sense must have known that we were coming."

Nobel Prize-winning physicist Charles Townes described why he thought fine-tuning pointed to the design of the universe by an intelligent Creator:

> Intelligent design, as one sees it from a scientific point of view, seems to be quite real. This is a very special universe: it's remarkable that it came out just this way. If the laws of physics weren't just the way they are, we couldn't be here at all. The sun couldn't be there, the laws of gravity and nuclear laws and magnetic theory, quantum mechanics, and so on have to be just the way they are for us to be here.
>
> Some scientists argue that "well, there's an enormous number of universes and each one is a little different. This one just happened to turn out right." Well, that's a postulate, and it's a pretty fantastic postulate—it assumes there really are an enormous number of universes and that the laws could be different for each of them. The other possibility is that ours was planned, and that's why it has come out so specially.[36]

Townes was a Christian, but Cambridge University physicist Fred Hoyle, who was an atheist, held a similar view. He famously declared that "a common sense interpretation of the facts suggests that a super-intellect has monkeyed with physics, as well as with chemistry and biology."[37]

Scientific Discovery #3: Information Drives Biology

I've already mentioned the third discovery: information at the basis of life. DNA operates like an information code, and in our experience, in all cases where we can definitively trace the source, information codes derive from minds, not unthinking matter. Stephen Meyer likes to cite information theorist Henry Quastler's observation that the "creation of information is habitually associated with conscious activity."[38] Interestingly, Quastler himself was trying to explain the origin of biological information through accidental material causes. But in the process, he inadvertently acknowledged that in our own experience, the creation of information was "habitually associated" with a mind.

The existence of information at the foundation of life has implications all the way up the line in the development of life, not just at the molecular level. If Meyer is right and an undirected process cannot generate the information required to build even a single protein, how much less would it be able to create the information needed for more complex things such as the novel animal body plans that arose during the event in the history of life known as the Cambrian Explosion?[39]

"To produce a new organism like a trilobite," explains Meyer, "... you need a whole bunch of new cell types; and... then you need new proteins to service the different unique cell types; and to build the proteins you need genetic information in the form of DNA."[40]

"The big question that the Cambrian Explosion poses," continues Meyer, "is where does all that new information come from? Where does the new information come from needed to build those proteins, to service those new cell types, to build these fundamentally new forms of animals?" Meyer argues that supporters of neo-Darwinism and scientific materialism "are really at a loss to answer that question. It's a sudden emergence of [a] huge amount of new information and really defies the capacity of the natural selection-mutation mechanism to produce all that information."[41] Instead, he concludes, the discovery of the wealth of information at the heart of all biological life, combined with our uniform experience regarding what does and does not create novel information, provides powerful evidence of the intelligent design of life by a Creator.

After reading Meyer's *Return of the God Hypothesis*, Nobel laureate physicist Brian Josephson at Cambridge University, had this to say: "This book makes it clear that far from being an unscientific claim, intelligent design is valid science."[42]

Thus we find that modern scientific findings strongly suggest the reality of nature's Creator. After being detoured by Darwin and others, science has returned to the wisdom of Thomas Jefferson: "I hold (without appeal to revelation) that when we take a view of the Universe, in its parts general or particular, it is impossible for the human mind not to perceive and feel a conviction of design, consummate skill, and indefinite power in every atom of its composition."[43]

The Case for Human Equality

Scientific findings have also revived the Founders' case for human equality. The evidence for human equality begins with human exceptionalism. For all of our differences, we humans as a group are much more like each other than we are to other animals. We possess unique features that put every normally developed human being in the same class apart from other living things. In the Bible's language, humans are uniquely "created in the image of God."

Darwin's theory of evolution, as we saw, tried to obliterate the fundamental difference between humans and other creatures. Darwinists claimed that human reason and language were not in principle different from the reasoning powers and methods of communication used by other animals. They insisted that the human development of technology was not in principle different from the use of sticks and stones by chimps and birds. They suggested that humans had no real free will and their brains were simply machines made of meat. They asserted that human morality could be explained away as the evolving product of natural selection and that whatever beliefs about religion or morality we have were programmed into us by evolution, typically because they promoted the survival and reproduction of our ancestors in their environmental niche and thus were preserved by natural selection.

Then there is the refrain repeated ad nauseam that humans are only about 1 percent different from chimps at the genetic level. If you go to the Smithsonian's National Museum of Natural History, signage will tell you that "you and chimpanzees [are] 98.8% genetically similar."[44] Science popularizer Bill Nye similarly claims, "As our understanding of DNA has increased, we have come to understand that we share around 98.8 percent of our gene sequence with chimpanzees."[45] The not-so-subtle implication is that humans in the end are not fundamentally different from chimps.

In 2025, Harvard primatologist Christine Webb published *The Arrogant Ape: The Myth of Human Exceptionalism and Why It Matters*, which recycled (yet again) the claim that humans are not unique or special.[46] Ironically, Webb began her book by quoting

Shakespeare—oblivious to the fact that Shakespeare himself is an obvious example of the difference between humans and every other known creature on Earth.[47]

Despite the continued cultural drumbeat against human uniqueness in the name of science, the actual discoveries of science in recent decades tell a far different story.

Speech and Language

Consider how humans communicate. Human speech depends not just on innate linguistic abilities, but also on physical features of the human body that allow humans to vocalize more complex sounds than other animals can. "Humans have a unique anatomy that supports our ability to produce complex language," writes anthropologist and linguist Philip Lieberman of Brown University.[48] In particular, the growth of the supralaryngeal vocal tract (SVT) in the first eight to ten years of human life creates a structure that "allow[s] humans to produce a range of sounds not possible for infants and nonhuman animals."

Human speech is also richly symbolic, allowing us to make connections between objects, experiences, and ideas. This ability for symbolic communication makes both the arts and the sciences possible. Through language, humans can develop and explain scientific theories. They can debate the meaning of life. They can investigate the past and plan for the future. Again, this is something that makes humans unique. In his book *The Symbolic Species,* neuro-anthropologist Terrence Deacon points out:

> Though we share the same earth with millions of kinds of living creatures, we also live in a world that no other species has access to. We inhabit a world full of abstractions, impossibilities, and paradoxes. We alone brood about what didn't happen, and spend a large part of each day musing about the way things could have been.... And slowly, over the millennia, we have come to realize that no other species on earth seems able to follow us into this miraculous place.[49]

A number of researchers have tried experiments to teach apes human-like language skills. For many, these experiments have also demonstrated just how unique humans are. One of the most famous of these experiments involved trying to teach sign language to chimpanzee "Nim Chimpsky" in the 1970s. Lead researcher Herbert Terrace initially thought that Nim Chimpsky was able to combine the signs he was taught "into simple sentences."[50] But on closer analysis, Terrace concluded otherwise. In his view, chimps couldn't create sentences because they really couldn't understand the *meaning* of words. They were simply responding to rewards.

Others ape researchers disagree, but what is not controversial is that humans show a superior capacity for complex social communication and learning. According to one study of young children and apes, "humans were already more skilled than both chimpanzees and bonobos at socio-cognitive tasks by the age of 2 years, and continued improving rapidly until 4 years." The apes, in contrast, "did not significantly improve."[51] Some researchers think humans' increased brain power is due to "looser genetic control" that allows us "to learn and adapt with more flexibility."[52]

Technological Advancement

Charles Darwin made much of the fact that chimps and other animals could fashion and use simple tools: "The chimpanzee in a state of nature cracks a native fruit, somewhat like a walnut, with a stone... The tamed elephants in India are well known to break off branches of trees and use them to drive away the flies."[53] Other animals can build simple structures.

Yet it is hard to see how these rudimentary capabilities undermine the reality of human uniqueness in the realm of technological advancement. Elephants break off branches. Humans invent and operate tractors, telephones, and trombones. Beavers construct dams out of logs and mud.[54] Humans built Hoover Dam, a modern marvel requiring over three million cubic yards of concrete.[55] Birds build nests. Humans built (and rebuilt) the Cathedral of Notre Dame.[56] In the words of G. K. Chesterton, "The very fact that a bird can get as far as building a nest, and cannot get any farther, proves that he has not a mind as man has a mind."[57] The history of human technological development

Figure 5.3. Comparison of animal vs. human technology.

from the dawn of civilization onward is a history that shows a sharp divergence between humans and other species. The amazing developments of the past century have only made the gap between humans other living creatures wider. Birds continue to build their nests. Humans build skyscrapers, spaceships, jet planes, and supercomputers.

Human technological advancement is not just a fluke of evolutionary history. As my friend biologist Michael Denton has taught me, it reflects the incredible fine-tuning of nature that made our planet fit for technology and humans fit for developing it.

An indispensable step was our harnessing the power of fire.[58]

The use of fire is so much a part of human culture that most of us probably don't give it a second thought. But the mastery of fire was one of the greatest turning points in human history, allowing the development of technologies on which our modern lives depend. Fire enabled ceramics, which led to the production of pottery, pipes, bricks, and tiles. Fire led to the creation of glass, which produced glassware, windows, plate-glass mirrors, and eye-glasses. Fire led to metallurgy, which allowed us to transform raw ore containing copper, iron, and other metals into utensils, weapons, and other tools, unleashing a steady stream of inventions in the millennia that followed, including nails, improved wheels, axes, chisels, spoked-wheel chariots, hand mills, the moldboard plow, water mills, steam turbines, internal combustion engines, automobiles, telegraphs, telephones, and computer chips, to name but a few. In short, humanity's mastery of fire was the initial breakthrough that opened the way to a succession of innovations leading to the world we know today. According to Denton, there is only one known planet in the universe designed to reap the benefits of fire: Earth. And there is only one known animal capable of harnessing the power of fire: humans.

In order for our planet to fully realize the life-giving powers of controlled fire, a multitude of precise and exacting conditions had to obtain. Here are just a few:

- Our planet needed the right kind of atmosphere, one that permits both the existence of fire and the existence of a biological creature capable of using it.

- But to get the right kind of atmosphere, our planet had to be just the right size. Only planets of the right size can possess an oxygen-rich atmosphere, which is required if you want to have both respiration and combustion.
- In order to harness the most important benefits of fire, our planet needed the right kind of fuel—fuel that can generate fires with sufficient heat. Working with iron typically requires heat in excess of 1,200 degrees Celsius. You can't achieve or maintain that sort of heat simply by burning grass, branches, or even logs. You need coal or charcoal or something equivalent. And the existence of such fuels depends on the flourishing of large woody plants. Those plants, in turn, are made possible by a molecule known as lignin. According to Denton, "without lignin, there would be no woody plants, no wood, no coal, no charcoal, no fire, no pottery, and certainly no iron and probably no other metals or metallurgy."
- For the use of fire to result in new technologies, nature also had to be seeded beforehand with compounds and elements with powers that could be unlocked by fire. Such materials don't have to exist. But they do, and on our planet, in abundance. According to Denton, it's as if the materials of nature themselves were prepared beforehand to facilitate our technological development.

Finally, to unlock the powers of fire you need one more thing: living creatures capable of making and using fire. And to be able to do that, those creatures must have bodies of just the right size and design. They need muscles of precisely the right strength. They need arms of sufficient length, and hands of sufficient dexterity. They require nerves that can transmit messages with the right speed. They need nerves of the right diameter. If our nerve fibers were the size of those in invertebrates, for example, our nerve cords couldn't fit inside our bodies.

According to Denton, "The only biological design of an organism that could handle a fire, make fire and regulate it, seems to be a biological being of a design very similar to our own—about our size, about our height, with our hands, with the strength sufficient to hew largish blocks of wood and to hew the ore from the rocks and such like."[59] He says he "can't think of any other design that would really work. Certainly an elephant won't work. Neither will a parrot. And certainly no aquatic organism, however intelligent. Dolphins are quite intelligent, but even a super-intelligent dolphin could never make a fire because it's living in the water, and it can't do anything on land."[60]

His conclusion? "You've got to be a terrestrial organism of about our size and build to make a fire. I think that's unique. I think we're unique. A chimp would have difficulty because they're not as manually dexterous as us… We are uniquely fit to make a fire."

Free Will and an Immaterial Mind

According to scientific materialists, humans do not possess free will to make decisions. Our choices are pre-determined by our heredity and environment and implemented by the neurons of our brain. As a popular psychology textbook in the 1990s explained, defenders of free will may claim "that people sometimes make decisions not controlled by their genetics, their past experiences, or their environment. But what is left besides genetics and environment?"[61] In the words of evolutionary biologist Jerry Coyne, we are simply "robots made out of meat."[62] Francis Crick, co-discoverer of the structure of DNA, proclaimed a similar view: "'You,' your joys and your sorrows, your memories and your ambitions, your sense of personal identity and free will, are in fact no more than the behavior of a vast assembly of nerve cells and their associated molecules."[63]

Neuroscientists in particular have claimed to have collected evidence that all of our choices are pre-determined by our brains. However, actual research into our brains does not prove that claim.

Pediatric neurosurgeon Michael Egnor points to classic experiments by neuroscientist Wilder Penfield on the brains of thousands of patients: "Penfield found, to his amazement, that while he could elicit a spectrum of movements, perceptions, memories, and emotions by stimulating the brain, he was never able to stimulate the *will* of the patient."[64] In Penfield's own words, "There is no place in the cerebral cortex where electrical stimulation will cause the patient to believe or decide."[65] According to Egnor, "Penfield concluded that the will, the sense of agency, is an immaterial power of the mind, not a material power of the brain."[66]

Egnor also highlights research by neurophysiologist Benjamin Libet. Libet's research is often taken as undermining free will because he showed that an unconscious brain wave (the "readiness potential") would occur "400 milliseconds *before* the subject was aware of an intention to act." This was taken by many to show that the physical brain "generated [the subject's] decision, *prior* to the subject's awareness."[67] The choice thus appeared to be "dictated by the brain. Free will, it seemed, was an illusion." But further research showed that when subjects were asked to veto a decision, "there was no new brain activity associated with the veto."[68] In other words, "The veto appeared to be free will, and there was no brain wave corresponding to it. It appeared an immaterial act of will."

Libet's results continue to be debated, but follow-up studies cast further doubt on those who would use his research to disprove free will. According to neuroscientist Cristi Cooper, further "experiments show that the readiness potential (RP) does not co-vary with the will (W) to act, ruling out a causal role of the RP on W, and that a decision to move does not cause a larger EEG negativity compared with a decision to not move, indicating that it must not be associated with preparation for movement at all."[69] In short, the case against free will has not been proven by neuroscience. Cooper quotes with approval the warning of two researchers: "When one comes to the issue of human agency, great caution should be used before drawing bold philosophical, political and social conclusions from neurological findings, whose correct interpretation and value are still extremely controversial."[70]

In their recent book *The Immortal Mind*, Egnor and co-author Denyse O'Leary pile on scientific evidence that humans possess an immaterial mind.

"Like many scientists, I had been trained to believe that the soul is a myth and the mind is nothing more than the brain—that is, a physical machine," writes Egnor. "… Yet the more I investigated, the more I discovered that these supposed findings of science were myths."[71]

There is no question that brain damage can impair mental operations. But in his career, Egnor has encountered patients missing up to half of their brains who function normally. "I've treated and cared for scores of kids who grow up with brains that are deficient and minds that thrive," he says. "It is entirely true that some people who are born with large parts of their brains missing are profoundly handicapped. But surely the remarkable thing is that *so many are not.*"[72] If "everybody who lacked a certain part of the brain was disabled in a specific way," the materialist view that the brain is merely a machine might be convincing. "But that's not at all what we see."[73]

Egnor and O'Leary also cite a growing body of research showing that severely brain-damaged individuals can still possess rational faculties, even when in deep comas or in so-called "vegetative" states. "That is why it is a maxim in intensive care nursing to never say anything in the room of a comatose patient that you wouldn't say to that person wide awake."[74] As a case in point, Egnor recounts the experience of "a colleague who was chastised by a formerly comatose patient for telling a joke in her room that was in poor taste!"

Perhaps most tantalizing of all are the experiences of patients whose hearts have stopped or brain waves ceased, who nevertheless recover and then give accurate reports of what was happening around them at the time they were supposed to be dead. These reports can include precise details that they could not have seen even had they been physically conscious. For example, one patient claimed to have floated up and out of the hospital building and observed a red shoe on the roof. The shoe turned out to be really there.[75] A young girl who regained consciousness accurately reported what was happening at her home while she was unconscious in the hospital, including the precise food her mother was making for dinner.[76] Philosopher of religion Gary Habermas has reviewed the data of hundreds of such Near Death Experiences (NDEs). He concludes that "there is… a large plethora of evidential cases that are backed by strong corroboration."[77]

NDEs supply powerful evidence that our minds are not identical to our physical brains. They may even provide corroboration of the age-old belief that human identify survives physical death.

Non-Evolved Morality

Humans are the only creatures on our planet who pass laws, debate moral codes, and reflect on right and wrong. Post-Darwin, many scientists tried to explain away human morality as another product of natural selection. In the words of philosopher Michael Ruse and evolutionary biologist E. O. Wilson, "Morality... is merely an adaptation put in place to further our reproductive ends.... In an important sense, ethics as we understand it is an illusion fobbed off on us by our genes to get us to cooperate."[78]

Yet the purported material origin of human morality remains a conundrum for scientific materialists. Moral teachings often encourage us to sacrifice our own survival needs for the benefit of others. It is hard to see why natural selection would favor such traits. Trying to get around this problem, some evolutionary biologists claim that natural selection acts on a group as a whole, so it can select traits that may be good for the individual's group even though the traits may be immediately detrimental to the individual.

That is an arguable claim, but even if it were true, it doesn't explain what we see in human society. Morality among humans not only includes duties to those inside our group (our family, our clan, our community, our nation). It also includes sacrificial heroism on behalf of individuals outside the hero's group, and claims of universal duties. Jesus, when asked "Who is my neighbor?," told the parable of the Good Samaritan (Luke 10:25–27) to emphasize our duties to those outside our group. The Declaration of Independence appeals to the idea that all human beings are created equal and have the same unalienable rights—not just Americans. In sum, even if in-group morality can be produced by natural selection, what about out-group morality? How are these kinds of universal moral claims explained by evolution?

I once led a private colloquium on evolution and morality featuring a group of elite academics. One participant was a very prominent evolutionary biologist known for advocating group selection to explain the development of morality. But even he conceded that his account did not explain out-group morality. He is not the only one who recognizes the problem. As two scholars who write about this area note, "The predominant evolutionary account of morality... leaves unexplained a number of important features of contemporary human morality—namely, the very cosmopolitan and other inclusivist moral commitments that prominent evolutionary explanations appear to rule out."[79]

The Myth of the 1 Percent Difference Between Humans and Chimps

Scientists have even overturned the widespread claim that humans are only 1 percent different from chimps in their DNA. According to research published in early 2025, "the actual difference between the human and chimp genomes turns out to be much greater than previously claimed," explains scientist Casey Luskin.[80] "Instead of 1 percent, it's between 14 to 14.9 percent. That's 14 times more than the often-quoted 1 percent statistic." The research showing this was published in *Nature*, arguably the world's most prestigious science journal.[81] Christine Webb apparently did not get the message. When her book debunking "The Myth of Human Exceptionalism" came out five months later, it continued to promote the now falsified claim that human and chimp genomes are 98.7 percent similar.[82]

So just like America's Founders believed, humans as a group share distinctive traits that make them equal as a class when compared to other animals. But what about differences *among* humans? As discussed in the previous chapter, for decades many Darwinian scientists regarded non-whites as lower on the evolutionary scale than whites, and a cottage industry developed in science trying to show the genetic inferiority of non-whites. Unfortunately, echoes of these poisonous claims persist today even among some who profess to be Christians.[83]

But, here again, science is now pointing in another direction, one that corroborates rather than undermines the biblical view that humans were created in the "image of God" and the Declaration of Independence's claim that "all men are created equal."

Genetically Equal

Recent science has undermined the idea that races or other groupings of humans are fundamentally different from each other at the genetic level. In truth, humans are more than 99 percent the same genetically speaking. According to the National Human Genome Research Institute, the genomes of any two individuals "are, on average, ~99.6% identical and ~0.4% different."[84]

Moreover, the vast majority of genetic variation that does exist among humans occurs *within* races and groups rather than *between* them. Researchers in 2002 reported that "within-population differences among individuals account for 93 to 95% of genetic variation; differences among major groups constitute only 3 to 5%."[85] A more recent study published in 2025 reaffirmed "that most genetic variance is within race and ethnicity groups… rather than between groups."[86] Other scientists discovered that "most variation in gene expression (92%) and splicing (95%) was distributed within versus between populations, which mirrored the variation in DNA sequence."[87]

This means that "for any given DNA sequence or gene, two individuals from different populations are sometimes more similar to one another than are two individuals from the same population."[88] UK geneticist Adam Rutherford explains: "Take two people, for example from Ethiopia and Namibia, and they will be more different to each other at a genetic level than either one of them is to a white European, or indeed a Japanese person, an Inuit or an Indian."[89]

"The fact that humans are relatively homogeneous at the DNA level, combined with the fact that between-population variation is modest, has significant social implications," argues University of Utah geneticist Lynn Jorde.[90] "Importantly, these patterns imply that the DNA differences between individuals, and between populations, are relatively scant and do not provide a biological basis for any form of discrimination."

For these and other reasons, most scientists now doubt the validity of treating popularly defined "races" as fundamental biological categories. In the words of the American Society of Human Genetics (ASHG), "although there are clear observable correlations between variation in the human genome and how individuals identify by race, the study of human genetics challenges the traditional concept of different races of humans as biologically separate and distinct. This is validated by many decades of research."[91]

The reality is that "there is considerable genetic overlap among members of different populations."[92] According to a consensus report published by the National Academies of Sciences, Engineering, and Medicine in 2025, "genetic variation overlaps across racial and ethnic groups instead of creating distinct clusters. A single racial category used in social and political contexts encompasses people with diverse genetic features. Combining these individuals into one group for scientific analyses can lead to oversimplification, misinterpretation, and inaccurate science."[93]

None of this is to deny that certain genetic variations may be found in particular populations of humans. But the relevant populations aren't typically identical with what most people refer to as races. As a group of sixty-seven scientists and other researchers pointed out in 2018, there is a "robust body of scholarship [that] recognizes the existence of geographically based genetic variation in our species, but [it] shows that such variation is not consistent with biological definitions of race. Nor does that variation map precisely onto ever changing socially defined racial groups."[94] The researchers cited sickle cell anemia as an example: "While it does have a high prevalence in populations of people with West and Central African ancestry, it also has a high prevalence in populations from much of the Arabian Peninsula, and parts of the Mediterranean and India. This is because the genetic variant that causes sickle cell is more prevalent in people descended from parts of the world with a high incidence of malaria. 'Race' has nothing to do with it."

The overlap of genetic variations between races makes sense in light of the diverse ancestry of current humans. According to research published in 2017, "the vast majority (97.3%) of individuals have mixed ancestry, with evidence of multiple ancestries in 96.8% of samples and on all continents. The data indicate that continents, ethno-linguistic groups, races, ethnicities, and individuals all show substantial ancestral heterogeneity."[95]

"Every Nazi has Jewish ancestors… Every white supremacist has Middle Eastern ancestors. Every racist has African, Indian, East Asian ancestors, as well as everyone else," says geneticist Adam Rutherford.[96] "Racial purity is pure fantasy. For humans, there are no pure bloods. Only mongrels enriched by the blood of multitudes." According to the American Society of Human Genetics, "it follows that there can be no genetics-based support for claiming one group as superior to another."

The bottom line? When it comes to genetics, humans as a whole are far more similar to each other than they are different, regardless of their race or ethnicity.

Intelligence Not Dictated by Heredity

What about human intelligence? Are some racial or ethnic groups biologically less fit than others in their native intellectual capabilities? This is an explosive topic, and for good reason. Past discussions in American history over possible differences in native intelligence between races/ethnicities were not merely abstract philosophical or scientific disputes. Many in America who developed and promoted IQ tests were joined at the hip with the eugenics movement, and IQ tests were used to justify rhetoric and public policies that demeaned and treated unfairly non-whites and whites of disfavored ethnic groups.[97] This unsavory background to the debates over "intelligence" doesn't necessarily mean that intelligence testing today has the same problems. But it does mean that we should be especially cautious when analyzing present-day claims that some races or ethnicities are superior in native intelligence to others.

In a review of ten years of "molecular genetic (DNA-based) research on intelligence," researchers in 2022 concluded:

> We barely have even a rudimentary understanding of how variation in the huge number of genetic variants identified as being associated with intelligence test scores and brain indices might directly relate to mechanisms (e.g. protein expression) and how these go on to facilitate the neurobiological machinery whose properties can be estimated and tested for any associations with differences

in general cognitive ability. The explanatory gap between genetic loci and cognitive test scores is massive.... Imaging and genetic variables account for a minority of intelligence variation.[98]

Other scholars have presented credible evidence that the results of IQ tests may reflect a variety of non-hereditary factors. For example, a 2010 study based on IQ data collected over several decades concluded that IQ rates vary over time and the measured differences are largely determined by underlying literacy rates: "This pattern of findings supports the hypothesis that both secular and racial differences in intelligence test scores have an environmental explanation: secular and racial differences in IQ are an artifact of variation in literacy skills. These findings suggest that racial IQ distributions will converge if opportunities are equalized for different population groups to achieve the same high level of literacy skills."[99]

In short, current science does not support the claim that different racial or ethnic groups have significant inborn and unchangeable differences in intelligence.

Behavior Not Dictated by Genes

Since the advent of modern genetics, the holy grail of behavioral research has been to demonstrate that our behaviors are dictated by our genes or biology, and massive government spending has been devoted to research premised on this idea. Yet despite perennial hype over genetic determinism, the scientific evidence does not support it, nor does it support the claim that different races or ethnic groups are genetically determined to engage in crime or other dysfunctional behaviors.

While certain biological differences may influence our susceptibility to certain kinds of behavior, research indicates that they do not in the end dictate complex behavioral traits like crime or sexual practices. As two criminologists point out, "The identified effects of genetic and biological factors on crime and related behaviors are consistently limited to the role of mediating or moderating the effects of environmental factors," and "the more we learn about biological and genetic influences and mechanisms, the more consequential and intertwined social influences become."[100]

Consider a study from 2019 that attempted "to construct a genome-wide measure of genetic propensity for aggressive behavior and use it to predict lifetime incarceration risk."[101] Researchers found that males "with a higher genetic propensity for aggression are more likely to experience incarceration." But they also discovered that the "genetic propensity is reduced, substantively and statistically, to a non-significant predictor for males raised in homes where at least one parent graduated high school."

Another study in 2018 looked at polygenic risks for low educational attainment and whether they were associated with criminal behavior later in life. While they found that "some children are born with genetic propensities that are associated with their risk to offend,"[102] they went on to say that their "findings do not support a view of genetics as destiny": "Many children who carry few education-associated alleles develop good behavioral control, complete schooling, and do not engage in delinquent behavior. Others develop behavioral problems, drop out of school, and become involved in crime. Alongside environmental factors, genetics explain a small proportion of these individual differences in life outcomes."

In a more comprehensive study from 2021, researchers reviewed "24 polymorphisms in genes related to human behavior previously associated with criminal behavior." They found that "no single variant is [cap]able of significantly modifying a specific phenotype." They concluded: "When human behaviour is considered as a phenotype, the lack of reproducibility of the genetic association data published so far, the weakness of statistical associations, the heterogeneity of the phenotype, and the massive influence of the environment on human behaviour do not allow us to consider these genetic variants as clearly associated with antisocial behaviour."[103]

Moreover, the researchers said that the "data support the absence of significant ethnic differences in molecular pathways that have been associated with aggressive and criminal behavior."[104] They continued: "While data on single polymorphic variants showed differential distribution across populations, these statistical differences were not confirmed when a comprehensive analysis was conducted on the total number of published variants. These data confirm the scientific assumption of the absence of biological races, even from a criminalistic point of view." In short, in the view of the researchers, "No person is born violent." Instead, "every person... acquires the possibility of developing violent behavior following exposure to environmental triggers."[105]

One doesn't need to be conversant with the latest research to understand that the idea of significant inborn/hereditary differences in behavior between racial or ethnic groups should be highly questionable—especially if one is searching for differences that are clear and large enough to shape public policies. Over the past century, there have been dramatic shifts in both crime and marriage rates in various racial/ethnic groups. These shifts have been so quick (in evolutionary terms) that it is impossible to claim with any cogency that the changes were largely due to heredity or the result of genetic programming. Cultural and environmental factors are vastly more likely.

Consider the rates of children born out of wedlock. While it is true that certain racial/ethnic groups have much higher rates of out-of-wedlock births than others, it is equally true that these rates have varied wildly over time.[106] The same is true with crime rates, which not only aren't dictated by genetics, but aren't even consistently associated with other material factors, such as economic distress.

The Great Depression was one of the worst economic turndowns America ever experienced. If economic distress necessarily drove people to crime, the Depression should have done it. Yet as Jeffrey Adler notes, violent crime actually plummeted in the 1930s in America:

> Nearly every kind of lethal violence plummeted, though the dip in male-on-male intraracial crime accounted for the overwhelming majority of the decrease. In New Orleans, the African American rate dropped by 64 percent and the white rate by 55 percent. Robbery-homicide rates fell by one-third, street homicide by one-half, and gun homicide by three-quarters. State-level data reveal similar trends. In Louisiana the homicide rate dipped by 46 percent among African American residents and by 45 percent

18

For every old blackboard
there are now hundredsof new electronic
computers.

THE PROSPECT of domination
of the nation's scholars by Federal
employment, project allocations,
and the power of money is ever present --
and is gravely to be regarded.

YET, in holding scientific research
and discovery in respect, as we should,
we must also be alert to the equal
and opposite danger that public policy
could itself become the captive
of a scientific-technological elite.

Figure 5.4. *Top:* President Dwight Eisenhower. *Bottom:* Page from Eisenhower's Farewell Address, where he warned about the rise of "a scientific-technological elite."

> among white residents. Illinois experienced a parallel reduction, with the African American rate shrinking by 67 percent and the white rate by 48 percent. In spite of the ravages of the Great Depression, on the eve of World War II the United States was the least violent it had been for at least four decades, confounding long-held (and enduring) assumptions about the relation of poverty and violence.[107]

When Thomas Jefferson suggested late in life that "the light of science" was showing "that the mass of mankind has not been born with saddles on their backs, nor a favored few booted and spurred, ready to ride them,"[108] he was more prophetic than he knew.

But if basic human equality is now supported rather than undermined by science, what does that mean for the progressive era claim that scientific elites should rule us for our own good without our consent?

COVID-19 and the Case for Consent of the Governed

As President Dwight Eisenhower prepared to leave office in January 1961, he delivered a Farewell Address to the nation that is best remembered today for its caution about a "military-industrial complex." But Eisenhower said something else that has been largely forgotten. He prophetically warned Americans of the "danger that public policy could... become the captive of a scientific-technological elite."[109]

During COVID-19, we saw Eisenhower's fearful prediction come true in real time. The COVID pandemic was used to justify an extraordinary expansion of government power in the name of science: lengthy "lockdowns" of businesses and churches, vaccination mandates, government-imposed discrimination against people based on their medical choices, government-encouraged censorship of dissenting scientific views, and more. Perhaps you supported some of these policies as necessary. Perhaps you didn't. But even if you supported each and every one of the policies adopted, you ought to be concerned by *how* they were imposed.

Almost none of the policies were enacted by legislative bodies after an open public debate. Almost all of the policies were enacted unilaterally by executive branch officials asserting emergency powers or by unelected public health officials immune from public accountability.[110]

By 2022, well after the COVID pandemic had subsided, there still were jurisdictions clinging to their emergency powers. In fact, the state of California did not end its "state of emergency" until the end of February 2023.[111]

Government officials learned during COVID how to do an end-run around America's normal system of checks and balances: Invoke "science" and declare an emergency—and then extend the emergency orders time and again. Anyone who dared challenge the emergency orders could be told they weren't scientists, so they had no right to be heard, and stigmatized as "anti-science" for good measure.

Medical doctor Anthony Fauci served as the longtime Director of the National Institute of Allergy and Infectious Diseases, and he became one of the government's main spokespersons for science during the pandemic. After facing public criticism, he responded irritably that any attack on him was indistinguishable from an attack on science itself: "A lot of what you're seeing as attacks on me, quite frankly, are attacks on science, because all of the things that I have spoken about, consistently from the very beginning, have been fundamentally based on science."[112]

Regardless of your view of specific COVID policies, the expansion of government power during the pandemic set a terrible precedent for the future.

Among the worst casualties of government overreach during COVID was free speech, one of the foundations of our constitutional system. Americans were told continuously that "misinformation" or "disinformation" had to be stopped.

No decent person favors the spread of "misinformation." But who is to judge what constitutes "misinformation"? Those warning of "misinformation" seemed to assume that existing elites are always right and so should be in charge of determining what is true or false, and which voices of "misinformation" must be silenced. But anyone conversant with the history of science or government knows that this claim can't hold up to scrutiny. Neither elite scientists nor government officials have a monopoly on the truth. Truth often arises from dissenters. That's why we have free speech in the first place.

Americans were also told that allowing free speech about COVID and related policies was too dangerous to permit. But the claim that speech is too dangerous to permit is always the go-to argument for totalitarians. If they had their way, we wouldn't have free speech about anything.

Arguments for censorship in the name of science had been made before regarding Darwinian evolution[113] and climate change.[114] But COVID-19 raised the lobbying for suppression to a whole new level. President Joe Biden and his Surgeon General actively pressured journalists and tech companies to censor messages disfavored by the government.[115] Taxpayer-funded National Public Radio all but urged medical licensing boards to strip medical licenses from doctors who offered dissenting opinions about COVID and its treatments.[116]

Tech companies even blocked citizen access to their elected officials' statements and deliberations about science and public policy. Public officials were banned or suspended by Twitter and Facebook for voicing their views. In one especially notorious case, hearings and expert panels convened by US Senator Ron Johnson from Wisconsin were repeatedly censored by YouTube because they featured scientists and experts who offer evidence-based critiques of current COVID policies.[117]

According to *The Washington Post*, the former head of the NIH, Francis Collins, believed we should "identify those who are purposefully spreading false information online and bring them to justice."[118] The CEO of Pfizer branded those circulating criticisms of his company's vaccines as "criminals because they have literally cost millions of lives."[119] Criminals. And criminals are supposed to be punished, right? Accordingly, a New York state legislator proposed a bill he said would "force social media companies to be held accountable for the dangers they promote" by allowing their users to express "disinformation" like "anti-vaccine falsehoods."[120] The bill would have authorized both government and private parties to seek court orders and damages against offenders.[121] In the words of law professor Jonathan Turley, "the New York legislation would gut free speech by creating criminal penalties for views deemed 'false' despite the continuing debates over issues like the efficacy of masks or vaccine protocols."[122]

In the fall of 2022, California actually enacted a COVID censorship bill to punish medical doctors who spread "misinformation" or "disinformation" about COVID-19.[123] But the fine print made clear that the law was a Trojan Horse. Its real concern was stopping dissent, not stopping falsehoods. This can be seen in the law's peculiar definition of "misinformation." According to the law, "misinformation" was not any kind of false information. It was only "false information that is contradicted by contemporary scientific consensus contrary to the standard of care." In other words, the only kind of "misinformation" penalized by the law was "false information" that disagreed with the "scientific consensus." False information that agreed with the consensus was to be left untouched.

Don't get me wrong: There definitely *was* misinformation in public discussions of COVID. Some of it came from private parties. Some of it came from government officials.[124] But lost in the debate over censorship was the fact that much so-called "misinformation" represented legitimate differences of opinion held by scientists and policy experts.[125] Other instances of supposed misinformation turned out to be true facts that those in charge preferred not to acknowledge or address.

For example, it is fact, not fiction, that the government's Vaccine Adverse Event Reporting System (VAERS) has had more adverse reaction reports filed for the COVID-19 vaccines than for any other vaccine since VAERS started collecting data in 1990.[126] By early October 2022, 62 percent of all adverse reactions, 68 percent of all hospitalizations, and 77 percent of all deaths reported to VAERS were associated with the COVID-19 vaccines. Correlation is not causation, and what this data meant was subject to legitimate differences of opinion. But the fact that the data existed was unquestionable. Yet if you spent much time discussing it in social media or on YouTube during the pandemic, you were likely to be banned.

The traditional way to combat misinformation in a free society is by encouraging the free exchange of ideas, not suppressing it. As John Milton famously argued, we are wrong to restrict free speech, misdoubting the strength of truth in open debate. "Let her [Truth] and Falsehood grapple; who ever knew Truth put to the worse, in a free and open encounter?"[127]

During COVID, a large part of America's ruling class repudiated that wise counsel.

Apart from censorship, the most worrisome aspect of public discussions during the pandemic was the use of science to justify dehumanization. Following past abuses of medical science in Nazi Germany and America, there developed strong support for a person's right to determine what medical treatments he or she receives. This was regarded as a fundamental human right. In less than two years, the pandemic obliterated that cultural consensus. As a result, there was a mass campaign to dehumanize an entire class of people because of their medical choices.

Fellow citizens who chose not to be vaccinated with the COVID vaccine were branded "narcissists," "child abusers" and "parasites."[128] They were accused of "killing off their fellow citizens."[129] They were denounced as "dangerous" people "from poorer or less educated parts of society."[130] They were described as "a leech on everyone else's participation in making America healthy and safe."[131] A sitting federal judge declared that "the vast majority of unvaccinated adults" were either (take your pick) "uninformed and irrational" or "selfish and unpatriotic."[132] A member of a famous rock band labeled them "an enemy" of society with a "delusional, evil idea."[133] A New York newspaper derided them as low in IQ.[134] The Republican governor of Alabama urged that "it's time to start blaming the unvaccinated folks," accusing them of embracing "a horrible lifestyle."[135] A former speechwriter for George W. Bush compared the unvaccinated to cancer, calling them "the malignant minority."[136]

This kind of "othering" in the name of science is repulsive.[137] The closest analogue I can think of to anything like this goes back to the social Darwinist eugenics movement in the early twentieth century, where eugenicists like Margaret Sanger succeeded in invoking science to sterilize people they similarly labeled "parasites," "leeches," "cancerous growths," and more.[138]

Sadly, even many religious leaders were silent about the dehumanization, or worse, they were complicit. Francis Collins, the nation's most noted evangelical Christian scientist, fanned the flames of hatred against the unvaccinated.[139] Evangelical political commentator David French lashed out at unvaccinated Christians for espousing views that are "extreme and dangerous" and for having "a hardened heart" where "reason and virtue have difficulty penetrating."[140]

The vicious rhetoric had cruel real-world consequences. Unvaccinated people lost their jobs and their livelihoods, often by government decree.[141] They were denied unemployment benefits—benefits they paid for through their payroll taxes.[142] Doctors announced that they would not serve unvaccinated people,[143] and unvaccinated patients were denied life-saving organ transplants.[144] Unvaccinated people were denied access to marriage licenses.[145] Judges tried to deny child visitation rights to parents who were not vaccinated.[146] In many jurisdictions healthy unvaccinated people were banned from stores, theaters, and sporting events.

Some pushed for even more draconian actions. In early 2022, the editorial board of the *Salt Lake City Tribune* opined that the government should "deploy the National Guard to ensure that people without proof of vaccination would not be allowed, well, anywhere."[147]

Plenty of Americans agreed. According to a national survey, many voters affiliated with one of America's main political parties all but abandoned their support for civil liberties in the fights against COVID.[148] Nearly 60 percent of them said that they "favor a government policy requiring that citizens remain confined to their homes at all times, except for emergencies, if they refuse to get a COVID-19 vaccine." Almost 50 percent thought "federal and state governments should be able to fine or imprison individuals who publicly question the efficacy of the existing COVID-19 vaccines on social media, television, radio, or in online or digital publications." Nearly the same amount said they "favor governments requiring citizens to temporarily live in designated facilities or locations if they refuse to get a COVID-19 vaccine."

These repressive measures were all justified in the name of "the science." But were they really based on science?

Consider the uncontroverted fact that millions of unvaccinated Americans had COVID-19 by the time the government was imposing vaccine mandates. According to research released in 2022 by the Centers for Disease Control, unvaccinated persons who already had COVID-19 were three times *less likely* to get COVID than *vaccinated* individuals who hadn't had COVID.[149] That's right—unvaccinated individuals who had COVID were far more protected than vaccinated individuals who hadn't. So there was absolutely no scientific basis for punishing or segregating the millions of unvaccinated people who had already had COVID. Yet the punitive policies targeting unvaccinated Americans made no distinction between those who had or hadn't had COVID, and the leading advocates for such policies didn't even attempt to explain why.

Or consider the push to compel COVID-19 vaccinations for children. Most children were at very low risk for death or serious complications from COVID-19,[150] so how was that push based on "the science"?

Or consider the effort to mandate vaccines for men under forty. According to a study conducted by the Florida Department of Health, there was "an 84% increase in the relative incidence of cardiac-related death among males 18–39 years old within 28 days following mRNA vaccination."[151] Is it really "the science" that dictated removing a young man's freedom to decide his own medical treatment?

As terrible as the government's overreach was during the pandemic, the resulting investigations proved a wake-up call for many Americans. At the end of 2024, the US House Select Subcommittee on the Coronavirus Pandemic issued a 557-page report.[152] It was scathing. It faulted government science officials for spreading misinformation about the origins of COVID-19, exaggerating the power of COVID-19 vaccines, and employing "Undemocratic and Likely Unconstitutional Methods to Fight What It Deemed to Be Misinformation."[153] The report also determined that "There Was No Quantitative Scientific Support for Six Feet of Social Distancing"[154] and "The U.S. Centers for Disease Control and Prevention Relied on Flawed Studies to Support the Issuing of Mask Mandates."[155]

Regarding the extended lockdowns imposed throughout America, the report concluded that "Unscientific COVID-19 Lockdowns Caused More Harm Than Good,"[156] itemizing their severe impacts on the economy, mental health, children, and young adults.

When it came to vaccine mandates, the report concluded that they too "Were Not Supported by Science,"[157] and "Caused Massive Collateral Damage and Were Very Likely Counterproductive."[158]

Other investigations have reached similar conclusions. A meta-analysis released in 2025 of twenty-two different studies determined that "lockdowns had a negligible effect on COVID-19 mortality."[159] Another study found that "incidents of domestic violence increased in response to stay-at-home/lockdown orders."[160] Still another study concluded that mask mandates on school children showed no positive benefit after the mandates persisted more than two weeks.[161] And there is growing controversy over the long-term efficacy and safety of the COVID-19 vaccines.[162]

Now, in the rear-view mirror, we can see more clearly why the principle of consent of the governed advocated for by America's Founders remains critically important. The massive failures of the scientific establishment during COVID provide powerful confirmation of the wisdom of the Founders. Experts are just as fallible and prone to abuse power as everyone else. That's why they must be held accountable to the people's representatives as well as to the Constitution. "All men are created equal" should mean at least this: Even experts should not be given unlimited authority. Even experts should be subject to the principles of the Declaration of Independence.

Fortunately, the government's overreach during COVID has spurred efforts to curtail the abuses. Some states eventually restricted the right of their governors to issue continuing emergency declarations without legislative consent.[163] Starting at the end of 2020, the US Supreme Court began curbing discriminatory restrictions on churches and religious worship.[164] In the fall of 2021, state and local government in California agreed to pay $800,000 to settle a religious liberty lawsuit over worship restrictions imposed on Grace Community Church in Los Angeles.[165]

COVID censorship policies also began to unravel. In 2023, California repealed its COVID "misinformation" law under the threat of more lawsuits. In 2024, Mark Zuckerberg of the social media giant Meta (owner of Facebook) apologized for his company's role in censoring debate during the pandemic. In a letter to the US House Committee on the Judiciary, Zuckerberg revealed, "In 2021, senior officials from the Biden Administration, including the White House, repeatedly pressured our teams for months to censor certain COVID-19 content, including humor and satire."[166] He added: "I believe the government pressure was wrong, and I regret that we were not more outspoken about it. I also think we made some choices that, with the benefit of hindsight and new information, we wouldn't make today." In 2025, Alphabet (owner of Google and YouTube) made its own admission that it had been pressured by the Biden administration to engage in censorship. By then, YouTube had already eliminated its specific policies restricting dissent over COVID, and it now announced an opportunity for reinstatement for accounts banned after repeatedly violating YouTube's previous COVID censorship policies.[167]

Also in 2025, Stanford University epidemiologist Jay Bhattacharya was appointed by President Trump to head the National Institutes of Health (NIH).[168] Bhattacharya was one of the scientists disparaged by former NIH-head Francis Collins after Bhattacharya co-authored the Great Barrington Declaration.[169] Written during the first year of the COVID-19 pandemic, the Declaration argued against lockdowns for everyone and suggested that public health policies should be focused on the most vulnerable instead. At the time, Collins privately dismissed the distinguished and well-published[170] Bhattacharya as a "fringe" epidemiologist.[171] A victim of censorship and blacklisting during COVID, Bhattacharya is committed to transparency and open debate in science.[172] Presumably he will help policymakers critically assess what we should do differently during the next pandemic.

To be sure, advocates of what Eisenhower called the "scientific-technological elite" have not gone away. Former NIH director Francis Collins continues to champion government by unelected experts. While acknowledging some government missteps during COVID, Collins advocates granting even more power to the federal public health bureaucracy.[173] He also argues that government efforts to control public debate during COVID didn't go far enough, incredibly suggesting that Communist China did a better job.

Thankfully, Collins has left government service and no longer possesses the power to implement such policies. Even so, many Americans still seem enamored by the idea that unelected experts should wield power rather than elected officials whom voters can hire or fire at the next election. In fact, more than three out of four Americans currently believe that "in our increasingly scientific and technological society, it is important to rely more on scientists and experts rather [than on] elected officials to decide public policy."[174]

Nevertheless, there are heartening signs that the questioning of scientific authoritarianism fueled by COVID policies is now expanding to other areas, such as so-called "gender affirming" care for minors.

When Children Are Abused in the Name of "Science"

In recent years, the World Professional Association for Transgender Health (WPATH) exerted enormous influence on government policies that authorize and fund sex-destructive treatments for children, including puberty blockers and surgeries to cut off breasts and other body parts.[175] WPATH justified its power grab by claiming to speak for science.

Dissenting doctors, scientists, parents, and lay activists raised serious questions about WPATH's recommendations for irreversible and destructive treatments for children, which they regarded as abuse. Using their rights as citizens, these activists persuaded a growing number of state governments to restrict sex-destructive medical treatments on minors.

Opponents of the reforms predictably cast them as anti-science. In 2024, *Scientific American* published a histrionic article critical of the new laws, titled "Pseudoscience Has Long Been Used to Oppress Transgender People."[176] The article's author tried to connect laws protecting children from mutilation to Nazi policies of murdering LGTBQ people. What is more interesting, however, is another connection the author made: "Prohibitions on gender-affirming care have occurred simultaneously with the relaxing of pandemic restrictions, and some scholars argue that the movement against trans health care is part of a broader movement aimed at discrediting scientific consensus." The author understood that the restoration of free speech over pandemic policies was having a wider impact.

In 2025, the US Supreme Court upheld the right of Tennessee to restrict sex transition treatments for minors. The concurring opinion by Justice Clarence Thomas was a tour de force in defending the right of government by consent of the governed rather than by unelected experts.

"When legislation does not cross constitutional lines, States must have leeway to effect the judgment of their citizens—no matter whether experts disagree," wrote Thomas. He added that when the Court in the past "has nonetheless given exalted status to expert opinion, it has been to our detriment."[177] His example was the infamous decision of *Buck v. Bell* (1927), where the court had upheld forced sterilization and helped place its imprimatur on the Darwinian eugenics movement.[178]

For Thomas, the application to the present was straightforward: "In politically contentious debates over matters shrouded in scientific uncertainty, courts should not assume that self-described experts are correct." He continued: "Deference to legislatures, not experts, is particularly critical here.... The Court today reserves 'to the people, their elected representatives, and the democratic process' the power to decide how best to address an area of medical uncertainty and extraordinary importance.... That sovereign prerogative does not bow to 'major medical organizations.'... '[E]xperts and elites have been wrong before—and they may prove to be wrong again.'"[179]

Thomas's concurring opinion signals that the progressive era's dream of replacing America's constitutional system with rule by unelected experts is no longer unchallenged.

The message of this chapter is that the eclipse of reality that placed the Declaration of Independence in shadow is ending. Once again, science is pointing to a Creator who endowed us with life and liberty, affirming the wisdom of the Bible and America's Founders. Science is again revealing how human beings are both equal and special, just as the Founders and the Bible professed. And the misuse of science during the COVID era is reawakening the resolve of many Americans to insist on government by consent rather than government by unelected elites.

The door to a return to the principles of America's Founding stands open. The question is whether we as a nation are willing to walk through it.

Figure 6.1. Statue of Abraham Lincoln (1809–1865) in the Lincoln Memorial, Washington, DC.

6. Where Do We Go from Here?

In the spring of 1836, a mob in St. Louis lynched Francis McIntosh, a free black man accused of murder. Without waiting for a trial, the mob kidnapped McIntosh, chained him to a tree, and burned him alive while he sang hymns.[1]

At the time, Abraham Lincoln was still in his twenties. Already a lawyer and state legislator,[2] he was horrified by the mob violence, and in January 1838 he courageously addressed it in a speech before the Young Men's Lyceum in Springfield, Illinois.

The stated theme of his remarks for the evening was "the perpetuation of our political institutions."[3] In a period of increasing lawlessness tied to politics, the topic couldn't have been more relevant.

Lincoln started by describing the "fundamental blessings" we inherited from the Founders: "We find ourselves under the government of a system of political institutions, conducing more essentially to the ends of civil and religious liberty, than any of which the history of former times tells us." We were not responsible for creating these institutions, he pointed out, and our only duty is to preserve them from attack and transmit them faithfully to our posterity.

Lincoln went on to argue that the primary danger America faced was not military. "All the armies of Europe, Asia and Africa combined... could not by force, take a drink from the Ohio, or make a track on the Blue Ridge, in a trial of a thousand years."

"At what point then is the approach of danger to be expected?" asked Lincoln. "I answer, if it ever reach us, it must spring up amongst us. It cannot come from abroad. If destruction be our lot, we must ourselves be its author and finisher. As a nation of freemen, we must live through all time, or die by suicide."

Lincoln's stirring words echo down through the ages. While America does face military threats, the danger of chaos from within still poses the most potent challenge.

The tumultuous 1960s was a time when great strides were made in civil rights, finally applying in no uncertain terms the principles of the Declaration of Independence to all races of Americans. But it was also a time when much of the rising generation seemed determined to overturn the wisdom of the past. It was during this period that Walt Disney took Lincoln's warning to heart, so much so that he made sure it was inserted into his "Great Moments with Mr. Lincoln" attraction at Disneyland. During a press preview, Disney told reporters that what Lincoln had to say "is a thing that we've got to listen to. I mean we don't need to worry about forces from the outside. It's the inside. Mass suicide he calls it. I agree with him."[4]

Today our nation is again torn by its divisions. Many Americans fundamentally disagree on the ends of government. Many more question whether America is even a legitimate nation. Lincoln's warning still applies.

I can think of no more fitting way to conclude this book than by recalling another speech by Lincoln. Two decades after his address to the Lyceum at Springfield, Lincoln was campaigning for the United States Senate seat held by Senator Stephen A. Douglas. He would ultimately lose that race, but just two years later, he would be elected president.

On a presumably hot and muggy August afternoon, Lincoln spoke in Lewiston, Illinois. More than two thousand crowded in front of the courthouse to hear him.[5] The correspondent for the *Chicago Press and Tribune* later reported, "This was truly one of the finest efforts of public speaking I ever listened to." He related that "the speech was two hours and a half long, yet there seemed to me to be more listeners at the conclusion than at the beginning."[6]

Lincoln ended his oration with an appeal to the Declaration of Independence.

Consider it his appeal to you, across the boundaries of time and place. Read it, and ponder what you can do to faithfully transmit our founding principles to your fellow Americans:

> Now, my countrymen... if you have been taught doctrines conflicting with the great landmarks of the Declaration of Independence; if you have listened to suggestions which would take away from its grandeur, and mutilate the fair symmetry of its proportions; if you have been inclined to believe that all men are *not* created equal in those inalienable rights enumerated by our chart of liberty, let me entreat you to come back. Return to the fountain whose waters spring close by the blood of the Revolution.
>
> Think nothing of me—take no thought for the political fate of any man whomsoever—but come back to the truths that are in the Declaration of Independence.
>
> You may do anything with me you choose, if you will but heed these sacred principles. You may not only defeat me for the Senate, but you may take me and put me to death. While pretending no indifference to earthly honors, I *do claim* to be actuated in this contest by something higher than an anxiety for office. I charge you to drop every paltry and insignificant thought for any man's success. It is nothing; I am nothing; Judge Douglas is nothing. *But do not destroy that immortal emblem of Humanity—the Declaration of American Independence.*[7]

Resources for Digging Deeper

I hope this book has whetted your appetite to learn more about the American Founding, the impact of scientific materialism on American culture, and the growing evidence of intelligent design in nature. If so, here are some resources for digging deeper. I don't necessarily agree with every point in every resource listed. But I recommend all of these resources as valuable explorations of some of the issues discussed in this book.

The American Founding (General)

- Harry Jaffa, ***A New Birth of Freedom: Abraham Lincoln and the Coming of the Civil War*** (Lanham, MD: Rowman and Littlefield, 2000). Nearly everything by the late Harry Jaffa is worth reading, and this book is one of his landmark works. Technically it is about the coming of the Civil War, not the American Founding. But Jaffa's view of the Founding is inextricably intertwined with this account.
- Thomas G. West, ***The Political Theory of the American Founding: Natural Rights, Public Policy, and the Moral Conditions of Freedom*** (New York: Cambridge University Press, 2017). A superb exploration of the political philosophy of America's Founders, which seeks to understand them as they understood themselves and draws out important implications of the Founders' views for today.

- Thomas G. West, ***Vindicating the Founders: Race, Sex, Class, and Justice in the Origins of America*** (Lanham, MD: Rowman and Littlefield, 1997). A helpful response to common attacks on the Founders as irredeemably racist, misogynist, plutocratic, and more.
- Matthew Spalding, ***The Making of the American Mind: The Story of Our Declaration of Independence*** (New York: Encounter Books, 2025). This book came out after I had finished a draft of my manuscript, but I had a chance to read it before I did my final edits. It's a splendid history of the writing of the Declaration and a wonderful exploration of its underlying philosophy. The book also provides an account of what happened later to the signers of the Declaration.
- John G. West, **"Political Philosophy of the Constitution,"** https://johngwest.com/1992/political-philosophy-of-the-constitution/. An article that explores how the Constitution was designed to promote virtuous leadership and good government.

The American Founding (Christian Influences On)

- John G. West, ***The Politics of Revelation and Reason: Religion and Civic Life in the New Nation*** (Lawrence, KS: University Press of Kansas, 1996). An exploration of the role of religion in the Founders' system and in the early years of the new nation.
- John G. West, **"Religion and the Constitution,"** https://johngwest.com/2001/religion-and-the-constitution/. An examination of the ways in which biblical ideas are reflected in the Constitution.
- Mark David Hall, ***Did America Have a Christian Founding?*** (Nashville: Thomas Nelson, 2020) and ***Proclaim Liberty Throughout the Land: How Christianity Has Advanced Freedom and Equality for All Americans*** (New York: Fidelis Books, 2023). Mark David Hall is probably the best living

scholar who focuses on the relationship between Christianity and the American Founding. If you want to know more about the Christian influences on the Founding, these two books are great places to start.

- Gary Amos and Richard Gardiner, ***Never Before in History: America's Inspired Birth*** (Richardson, TX: Foundation for Thought and Ethics, 1998). Originally intended for high school students, this textbook documents the Christian influences on early American history that most people don't know about.

The Impact of Science on American Culture

- John G. West, ***Darwin Day in America: How Our Politics and Culture Have Been Dehumanized in the Name of Science***, expanded paperback edition (Wilmington, DE: ISI Books, 2015). A sweeping exploration of the past and present impact of Darwinism and scientific materialism on American public policy and culture, including criminal justice, economics, welfare policy, architecture, education, sexuality, and bioethics.
- ***Human Zoos: America's Forgotten History of Scientific Racism*** (Seattle: Discovery Institute, 2018). An award-winning documentary exploring the history of Darwinian racism and eugenics in America from the nineteenth century to the present.
- Phillip E. Johnson, ***Reason in the Balance: The Case Against Naturalism in Science, Law & Education*** (Downers Grove, IL: InterVarsity Press, 1995). A classic and perceptive work by Berkeley law professor Phillip Johnson that examines the stranglehold of scientific naturalism on law, science, and education. Still relevant today.
- Wesley J. Smith, ***The War on Humans*** (Seattle: Discovery Institute Press, 2014) and ***The War on Humans*** documentary (2014), https://waronhumans.com/. A leading bioethicist examines the growing anti-human ideology of some environmentalists.

Evidence for Design and Purpose in Nature

- Stephen C. Meyer, ***Return of the God Hypothesis: Three Scientific Discoveries That Reveal the Mind Behind the Universe*** (New York: HarperOne, 2021). A magisterial yet accessible presentation of the accumulating scientific evidence that points to a Creator of the universe and of life. One of the most convincing arguments you will ever read.
- Michael Egnor and Denyse O'Leary, ***The Immortal Mind: A Neurosurgeon's Case for the Existence of the Soul*** (New York: Worthy Publishing, 2025). A powerful investigation of the evidence that humans possess a rational soul that survives death.
- Michael Denton, ***The Miracle of Man: The Fine Tuning of Nature for Human Existence*** (Seattle: Discovery Institute Press, 2022), and ***Fire-Maker: How Humans Were Designed to Harness Fire and Transform Our Planet*** (Seattle: Discovery Institute Press, 2016). If you want to increase your wonder of the natural world and better understand man's place in it, read biologist Michael Denton. He makes a compelling scientific case that nature is uniquely fit not only for life, but for creatures with human capabilities and design.
- William Dembski, ***The Design Revolution*** (Downers Grove, IL: InterVarsity Press, 2004) and William Dembski and Winston Ewert, ***The Design Inference: Eliminating Chance through Small Probabilities***, second edition, revised and expanded (Discovery Institute Press, 2023). Mathematician and philosopher William Dembski is one of the founding fathers of the modern intelligent design movement within the scientific community. Read the first book if you want an accessible yet comprehensive introduction to the theory of intelligent design while still in its early years. Read the second book (originally published with Cambridge University Press) if you are ready to explore a rigorously mathematical method for detecting intelligent causes in the world.

- Stuart Burgess, ***Ultimate Engineering: An Engineer Investigates the Biomechanics of the Human Body*** (Seattle: Discovery Institute Press, 2026). An award-winning engineer examines the amazing engineering of the human body and responds to those who argue that the human body is poorly designed thanks to evolution.
- ***Science Uprising***, https://scienceuprising.com/. A video series exploring various kinds of evidence for the intelligent design of nature and of human beings. Topics covered include the Big Bang, fine-tuning, human evolution, the DNA code, mutations, and artificial intelligence.
- ***Secrets of the Human Body***, https://secretsofthehumanbody.com/. A video series exploring the intelligent design and engineering of the human body.

Endnotes

Chapter 1: America's Creed

1. G. K. Chesterton, "What Is America?," in *What I Saw in America* (London: Hodder and Stoughton, 1922), *Project Gutenberg*, https://www.gutenberg.org/ebooks/27250.
2. "Declaration of Independence: A Transcription," *National Archives*, accessed December 15, 2025, https://www.archives.gov/founding-docs/declaration-transcript. For an important discussion of the punctuation of the Declaration, see Danielle Allen, *Our Declaration: A Reading of the Declaration of Independence in Defense of Equality* (New York: Liveright Publishing, 2014), Kindle, 278–281.
3. Letter of Charles Carroll of Carrollton, written in August 1826, published in *Niles' Weekly Register*, July 19, 1828, reprinted in *Niles' Weekly Register* (Baltimore: Niles and Son, undated) 34: 330. Carroll starts his letter by expressing his gratitude "to Almighty God for the blessings which through Jesus Christ our Lord he has conferred on my beloved country in her emancipation, and upon myself in permitting me, under circumstances of mercy, to live to the age of eighty-nine years, and to survive the fiftieth year of American Independence" (34: 329). Carroll would live until November 14, 1832.
4. Abraham Lincoln, "Speech on the Dred Scott Decision at Springfield Illinois" (Springfield, IL, June 26, 1857), *Abraham Lincoln: Speeches and Writings, 1832–1858* (New York: Library of America, 1989), 398, emphasis in the original.
5. See Lucas E. Morel, *Lincoln and the American Founding* (Carbondale, IL: Southern Illinois UP, 2020), esp. chap. 2, "Lincoln and the Declaration of Independence."
6. See Martin Luther King, Jr., "The American Dream" (Ebenezer Baptist Church, Atlanta, GA, July 4, 1965), https://www.rev.com/transcripts/the-american-dream-july-4th-speech-transcript-martin-luther-king-jr.
7. See "Lenin's Mausoleum," *Wikipedia*, last modified November 29, 2025, https://en.wikipedia.org/wiki/Lenin%27s_Mausoleum; "Chairman Mao Memorial Hall," *Wikipedia*, last modified November 15, 2025, https://en.wikipedia.org/wiki/Chairman_Mao_Memorial_Hall; "Ho Chi Minh Mausoleum," *Wikipedia*, last modified November 20, 2025, https://en.wikipedia.org/wiki/Ho_Chi_Minh_Mausoleum; and "Kumsusan Palace of the Sun," *Wikipedia*, last modified October 28, 2025, https://en.wikipedia.org/wiki/Kumsusan_Palace_of_the_Sun.
8. Mary Lynn Ritzenthaler and Catherine Nicholson, "The Declaration of Independence and the Hand of Time," *Prologue Magazine*, Fall 2016, https://www.archives.gov/publications/prologue/2016/fall/declaration.

9. "The Declaration of Independence: A History," *National Archives*, accessed December 15, 2025, https://www.archives.gov/founding-docs/declaration-history.
10. "1776–1876: After One Hundred Years, the Real Centennial Anniversary," *The Philadelphia Inquirer*, July 5, 1876, 1.
11. "1776–1876: After One Hundred Years," 1.
12. "The 'Declaration of Rights of the Women of the United States,'" *National Park Service*, accessed December 15, 2025, https://www.nps.gov/articles/the-declaration-of-rights-of-the-women-of-the-united-states.htm.
13. "The Declaration of Independence: A History."
14. "The Declaration of Independence: A History."
15. "Jefferson Memorial Dedication Drew Dignitaries, Declaration," *National Park Service*, accessed December 15, 2025, https://www.nps.gov/articles/jeffersondedication.htm.
16. "The Declaration of Independence: A History."
17. Larry Wines, "The 1947–1949 Freedom Train: The Train's Journey Across America," accessed December 15, 2025, https://www.freedomtrain.org/freedom-train-story-05-journey.htm.
18. According to the Newspapers.com database, the phrase "all men are created equal" has appeared in American newspapers more than 330,000 times. Search run on January 9, 2026.
19. Calvin Coolidge, "Declaration on Independence Anniversary Commemoration" (Independence Hall, Philadelphia, PA, July 5, 1926), https://millercenter.org/the-presidency/presidential-speeches/july-5-1926-declaration-independence-anniversary-commemoration.
20. Barack Obama, "Second Inaugural Address" (US Capitol, Washington, DC, January 21, 2013), https://millercenter.org/the-presidency/presidential-speeches/january-21-2013-second-inaugural-address.
21. *Mr. Smith Goes to Washington*, directed by Frank Capra (Columbia Pictures, 1939), https://www.imdb.com/title/tt0031679/.
22. *Prelude to War* (United States Army Signal Corps, 1942), https://www.imdb.com/title/tt0035209/.
23. *Ben and Me*, directed by Hamilton Luske, Clyde Geronimi, and Wilfred Jackson (Walt Disney Animation Studios, 1953), https://www.imdb.com/title/tt0045550/.
24. "Independence Hall," Knott's Berry Farm, accessed December 15, 2025, https://www.sixflags.com/knotts/attractions/independence-hall; Werner Weiss, "Independence Hall," accessed December 15, 2025, Yesterland.com, https://yesterland.com/independence.html.
25. For play, see "1776 (musical)," *Wikipedia*, last modified December 15, 2025, https://en.wikipedia.org/wiki/1776_(musical); for film, see "1776," IMDb, accessed December 15, 2025, https://www.imdb.com/title/tt0068156/.
26. *Scarecrow and Mrs. King*, season 3, episode 1, "A Lovely Little Affair," directed by Harvey S. Laidman, aired September 23, 1985, https://www.imdb.com/title/tt0695457/; David R. Johnson, Taya Johnston, and Sabine Ludewig, *The Ultimate Fan's Guide to Scarecrow and Mrs. King* (DRG Digital Media, 2023), 118; "The New Season: Week 1," *The Miami Herald*, October 2, 1985, https://www.newspapers.com/article/the-miami-herald/68417159/.

27. *National Treasure*, directed by Jon Turteltaub (Disney, 2004), https://www.imdb.com/title/tt0368891; "North America (US and Canada) Domestic Movie Chart for 2004," *The Numbers*, https://www.the-numbers.com/market/2004/top-grossing-movies.
28. This book does not cover all of the intellectual influences on the Founding, nor is it intended to offer a detailed discussion of the Founders' system of government. If you want to dig deeper into the Founders' philosophy and practice, an excellent place to start is Thomas G. West, *The Political Theory of the American Founding: Natural Rights, Public Policy, and the Moral Conditions of Freedom* (New York: Cambridge UP, 2017). Although I know Dr. West, we are not related (that we know of!).
29. John G. West, *How Americans View the American Founding* (Discovery Institute, 2026), 8, 10, 11, https://endowedbyourcreator.com/survey.
30. Nikole Hannah-Jones, "Our Democracy's Founding Ideals Were False When They Were Written. Black Americans Have Fought to Make Them True," *The New York Times Magazine*, August 14, 2019, https://www.nytimes.com/interactive/2019/08/14/magazine/black-history-american-democracy.html.
31. "Face Off: Christopher Rufo vs. Curtis Yarvin," *IM—1776*, April 11, 2024, https://im1776.com/2024/04/11/rufo-vs-yarvin/, emphasis in original.
32. Mencius Moldbug [Curtis Yarvin], "A Gentle Introduction to Unqualified Reservations, Chapter 2: The American Rebellion," *Unqualified Reservations*, January 15, 2009, https://www.unqualified-reservations.org/2009/01/gentle-introduction-to-unqualified_15/.
33. Mencius Moldbug [Curtis Yarvin], "How Dawkins Got Pwned, Chapter 3: *Manitou* and the *Zeitgeist*," *Unqualified Reservations*, October 11, 2007, note 4, https://www.unqualified-reservations.org/2007/10/how-dawkins-got-pwned-part-3/#cha-0_footnote-4.
34. Patrick J. Deneen, *Conserving America? Essays on Present Discontents* (South Bend, IN: St. Augustine's Press, 2016), 10. For Deneen's religious identification, see "Patrick Deneen on the Failure of Liberalism and the Importance of Relational Living," *Theos*, June 14, 2023, https://www.theosthinktank.co.uk/comment/2023/06/14/patrick-deneen-on-the-failure-of-liberalism-and-the-importance-of-relational-living.
35. Deneen, *Conserving America?*, 3.
36. Mangalwadi's views are covered in Chapter 2.
37. Julie Miller, "'A Republic if You Can Keep It': Elizabeth Willing Powel, Benjamin Franklin, and the James McHenry Journal," *Unfolding History*, Library of Congress, January 6, 2022, https://blogs.loc.gov/manuscripts/2022/01/a-republic-if-you-can-keep-it-elizabeth-willing-powel-benjamin-franklin-and-the-james-mchenry-journal/.

Chapter 2: We Hold These Truths

1. John Locke, *Two Treatises of Government* [1690]: *A Critical Edition with an Introduction and Apparatus Criticus by Peter Laslett,* rev. ed. (New York: New American Library, 1965), Book II, section 195; also see Book I, sections 93 and 126; Book II, sections 66 and 142.

2. Richard Hooker, *Of the Laws of Ecclesiastical Polity* [1594–1597], Book III, Chapter IX, section 2, in *The Works of That Learned and Judicious Diving Mr. Richard Hooker*, 7th ed. (Oxford: Clarendon Press, 1888).
3. Thomas Aquinas, *Treatise on Law* [circa 1270] (Chicago: Regnery Gateway, undated), Question 95, Article 3, 81.
4. Thomas Jefferson to Henry Lee, May 8, 1825, *National Archives: Founders Online*, https://founders.archives.gov/documents/Jefferson/98-01-02-5212.
5. James Wilson, *Lectures on Law*, in *Collected Works of James Wilson*, ed. Kermit L. Hall and Mark David Hall (Indianapolis, IN: Liberty Fund, 2007), I: 498.
6. George Washington to Henry Knox, March 2, 1797, *Writings of George Washington*, ed. John Fitzpatrick (Washington, DC: United States George Washington Bicentennial Commission, 1931–1944), XXXV: 409.
7. George Washington, "General Orders," July 29, 1779, *Writings*, XVI: 13.
8. George Washington to Benedict Arnold, September 14, 1775, *Writings*, III: 492.
9. John Adams, "A Dissertation on the Canon and the Feudal Law, No. 2," August 1765, *Papers of John Adams*, ed. Robert Taylor (Cambridge, MA: Belknap Press, 1977), I: 115.
10. Adams, "A Dissertation," August 1765, *Papers*, I: 116.
11. Adams, "A Dissertation," I: 116.
12. John Adams, "Discourses on Davila," 1790, *Works of John Adams*, ed. Charles Francis Adams (Boston, MA: Little, Brown, 1856), VI: 397.
13. John Jay, "Address to the American Bible Society," May 8, 1823, *Correspondence and Public Papers of John Jay*, ed. Henry Johnston (New York: Putnam's Sons, 1890–1893), IV: 488.
14. James Madison, "Madison's 'Detached Memoranda,'" *William and Mary Quarterly* 3 (1946): 560–561.
15. Alexander Hamilton, *The Farmer Refuted*, *The Papers of Alexander Hamilton*, ed. Harold C. Syrett (New York: Columbia UP, 1961–1979), I: 87.
16. Thomas Jefferson to James Fishback, September 27, 1809, *Jefferson's Extracts from the Gospels*, ed. Dickinson W. Adams (Princeton, NJ: Princeton UP, 1983), 343. Jefferson was so impressed by the moral teachings of Jesus that he created his own version of the New Testament commonly known today as the "Jefferson Bible." Its actual title was "The Life and Morals of Jesus of Nazareth." See "Thomas Jefferson's Bible," *National Museum of American History*, https://americanhistory.si.edu/JeffersonBible/history/index.cfm#1.
17. Unless otherwise noted, biblical quotations use the English Standard Version (ESV).
18. Because the standard English translations of this passage by Augustine are rather clunky, this is my own close paraphrase of Augustine. The translation I adapted can be found in Saint Augustin, Psalm LVIII, *Expositions on the Book of Psalms*, ed. A. Cleveland Coxe (American edition of the original, from Edinburgh: T&T Clark, circa 1885), available online at https://ccel.org/ccel/schaff/npnf108.all.html.
19. Thomas Aquinas, Prima Secundae Partis, Question 91, Art. 2, *The Summa Theologiae of St. Thomas Aquinas*, online edition by Kevin Knight based on the second and revised edition of 1920 by The Fathers of the English Dominican Province, https://www.newadvent.org/summa/2091.htm.

20. Martin Luther, "How Christians Should Regard Moses" [1525], *Martin Luther's Basic Theological Writings*, ed. Timothy F. Lull (Minneapolis, MN: Fortress Press, 1989), 142.
21. John Calvin, *Institutes of the Christian Religion*, Book IV, Chapter XX, section 16, trans. Henry Beveridge (Grand Rapids, MI: Eerdmans, 1989), 664.
22. C. S. Lewis, *Mere Christianity* (New York: Macmillan, 1960) and *The Abolition of Man* (New York: Macmillan, 1955). Martin Luther King, Jr. defended the natural law in his famous "Letter from Birmingham Jail," April 16, 1963, https://letterfromjail.com/.
23. Wilson, *Lectures on Law*, I: 603–604, II: 821.
24. Alexander Hamilton, "No. 31," in James Madison, Alexander Hamilton, John Jay, *The Federalist Papers*, ed. Clinton Rossiter (New York: New American Library, 1961), 193.
25. Thomas G. West, *The Political Theory of the American Founding: Natural Rights, Public Policy, and the Moral Conditions of Freedom* (New York: Cambridge UP, 2017), Kindle, 78; also see Hamilton, "No. 31," *The Federalist Papers*, 193.
26. Michael P. Zuckert, "Self-Evident Truth and the Declaration of Independence," *The Review of Politics* 49, no. 3 (Summer 1987): 322.
27. Quotations from Mangalwadi come from "An Interview with Vishal Mangalwadi," interview by Glenn Sunshine and John West, *Theology Pugcast*, November 18, 2024, episode 316, video, 1:06:16, https://www.youtube.com/watch?v=hxAfZVcngYA. This podcast was taped during the Post Tenebras Lux Conference on November 1, 2024, at Evangelical Reformed Church, Tacoma, WA.
28. Massimo Pigliucci, "Self-Evident: How Benjamin Franklin's Two-Word Edit Changed American History," *Figs in Winter: A Community of Reason*, January 15, 2025, https://figsinwintertime.substack.com/p/self-evident-how-benjamin-franklins.
29. Vishal Mangalwadi, "The Legacy of William Carey: A Model for the Transformation of a Culture," November 23, 2024, video, 50:29, https://www.youtube.com/watch?v=-AdfunnJE7Y. This lecture was taped during the Post Tenebras Lux Conference on November 2, 2024, at Evangelical Reformed Church, Tacoma, WA.
30. Walter Isaacson, "Declaring Independence: How They Chose These Words," *TIME*, July 7, 2003, https://time.com/archive/6596481/declaring-independence-how-they-chose-these-words/. Isaacson repeats his claim about Franklin in his most recent book, *The Greatest Sentence Ever Written* (New York: Simon and Schuster, 2025), Kindle, vi.
31. "III. Jefferson's 'Original Rough Draft' of the Declaration of Independence, 11 June–4 July 1776," *National Archives: Founders Online*, note 2, https://founders.archives.gov/documents/Jefferson/01-01-02-0176-0004#TSJN-01-01-0188-fn-0002.
32. Julian P. Boyd, *The Declaration of Independence: The Evolution of the Text* (Princeton, NJ: Princeton UP, 1945), 22.
33. For a discussion of the religious views of Jefferson, Franklin, and Adams, see my book *The Politics of Revelation and Reason: Religion and Civic Life in the New Nation* (Lawrence, KS: University Press of Kansas, 1996), 15–25, 49-–53, 56–67.

34. Thomas Jefferson to James Madison, August 30, 1823, *National Archives: Founders Online*, https://founders.archives.gov/documents/Jefferson/03-20-02-0123.
35. See "Religious Affiliation of the Signers of the Declaration of Independence," December 2005, https://freerepublic.com/focus/news/2546951/posts; William B. Miller, "Presbyterian Signers of the Declaration of Independence," *Journal of the Presbyterian Historical Society (1943–1961)* 36, no. 3 (September 1958):129–171; Mark David Hall, *Roger Sherman and the Creation of the American Republic* (New York: Oxford UP, 2013), 22.
36. "A total of 47 alterations, including the insertion of three complete paragraphs, were made to the text before it was presented to Congress on June 28. After voting for independence on July 2, Congress continued to refine the document, making 39 additional revisions to the committee draft before its final adoption on the morning of July 4." Gerard W. Gawalt, "Jefferson and the Declaration: Updated Work Studies Evolution of Historic Text," *Library of Congress: Information Bulletin*, July 1999, https://www.loc.gov/loc/lcib/9907/jeffdec.html.
37. Hall, *Roger Sherman*, 33–40; Lewis Henry Boutell, *The Life of Roger Sherman* (Chicago: A. C. McClurg and Co., 1896), 272–273.
38. John Witherspoon, *An Annotated Edition of Lectures on Moral Philosophy*, ed. Jack Scott (East Brunswick, NJ: Associated University Presses, 1982), 65.
39. John G. West, *How Americans View the American Founding* (Discovery Institute, 2026), 8, https://endowedbyourcreator.com/survey.
40. Depending on the characteristic of equality under discussion, 38–63 percent of American adults have a grasp of the kind of equality the Founders were talking about. That number goes down among Americans ages 18–34. See West, *How Americans View the American Founding*, 8–9, 16.
41. Charles Adams to John Adams, February 17, 1794, *National Archives: Founders Online*, https://founders.archives.gov/documents/Adams/04-10-02-0007-0006.
42. John Adams to Charles Adams, February 24, 1794, *National Archives: Founders Online*, https://founders.archives.gov/documents/Adams/04-10-02-0007-0007.
43. Wilson, *Lectures on Law*, I: 636.
44. John Adams to Charles Adams, February 24, 1794.
45. John Adams to Charles Adams, January 9, 1794, *National Archives: Founders Online*, https://founders.archives.gov/documents/Adams/04-10-02-0007-0003.
46. Witherspoon, *Lectures on Moral Philosophy*, 67.
47. Wilson, *Lectures on Law*, I: 585.
48. Wilson, *Lectures on Law*, I: 600.
49. Wilson, *Lectures on Law*, I: 587.
50. Wilson, *Lectures on Law*, I: 588.
51. Witherspoon, *Lectures on Moral Philosophy*, 78.
52. Wilson, *Lectures on Law*, I: 511.
53. Wilson, *Lectures on Law*, I: 512.
54. Thomas Jefferson to Thomas Law, June 13, 1814, *National Archives: Founders Online*, https://founders.archives.gov/documents/Jefferson/03-07-02-0307.
55. Jefferson to Law, June 13, 1814. Jefferson's lack of capitalization in places has been revised to match current practice.
56. Witherspoon, *Lectures on Moral Philosophy*, 67.

57. Wilson, *Lectures on Law*, I: 590.
58. James Madison, "No. 51," *The Federalist Papers*, 322.
59. Samuel James Smith, "The New-England Primer," *Britannica*, accessed December 26, 2025, https://www.britannica.com/topic/The-New-England-Primer; *The New-England Primer: A Reprint of the Earliest Known Edition, with Many Facsimiles and Reproductions, and an Historical Introduction*, ed. Paul Leicester Ford (New York: Dodd, Mead and Company, 1899), https://dn790002.ca.archive.org/0/items/newenglandprimer00fordiala/newenglandprimer00fordiala.pdf.
60. John Cotton, "Limitation of Government" (sermon, 1655), in *The Puritans: A Sourcebook of Their Writings*, rev. ed., eds. Perry Miller and Thomas H. Johnson (New York: Harper Torchbooks, 1963), I: 213.
61. Sydney Ahlstrom, *A Religious History of the American People* (New Haven, CT: Yale UP, 1972), 363.
62. John Adams to John Taylor, December 17, 1814, *National Archives: Founders Online*, https://founders.archives.gov/documents/Adams/99-02-02-6371.
63. Harry Jaffa, *A New Birth of Freedom: Abraham Lincoln and the Coming of the Civil War* (Lanham, MD: Rowman and Littlefield, 2000), 106.
64. Wilson, *Lectures on Law*, I: 638.
65. Alexander Hamilton, *The Farmer Refuted*, February 1775, *National Archives: Founders Online*, https://founders.archives.gov/documents/Hamilton/01-01-02-0057.
66. Benjamin Rush, *A Defence of the Use of the Bible in Schools* (New York: American Tract Society, undated), https://archive.org/details/bibleschool_202001/mode/2up, 11.
67. Wilson, *Lectures on Law*, I: 636.
68. "God created man in his own image; in the image of God created he him: male and female created he them. And God blessed them; and God said unto them, be fruitful and multiply, and replenish the earth, and subdue it: and have dominion over the fish of the sea, and over the fowl of the air, and over every living thing that moveth upon the earth." James Wilson, "On the History of Property," *Collected Works*, I: 387.
69. John Adams to Charles Adams, January 9, 1794, *National Archives: Founders Online*, https://founders.archives.gov/documents/Adams/04-10-02-0007-0003.
70. Thomas Paine, *Rights of Man: Being an Answer to Mr. Burke's Attack on the French Revolution*, 2nd ed. (London: J. S. Jordan, 1791), 49.
71. Paine, *Rights of Man*, 50.
72. Thomas Jefferson to Roger C. Weightman, June 24, 1826, "Declaring Independence: Drafting the Documents," *Library of Congress*, https://www.loc.gov/exhibits/declara/rcwltr.html.
73. Cicero, *De Natura Deorum*, II.xliv.115, trans. H. Rackham (Cambridge, MA: Harvard UP, 1929), 233.
74. See John G. West, *Stockholm Syndrome Christianity* (Seattle: Discovery Institute Press, 2025), 56–58; *Design in the Bible and the Early Church Fathers* (Seattle: Discovery Institute, 2009); *The Patristic Understanding of Creation: An Anthology of Writings from the Church Fathers on Creation and Design*, eds. William A. Dembski, Wayne J. Downs, and Father Justin B. A. Frederick (Riesel, TX: Erasmus Press, 2008).

75. Thomas Aquinas, *Summa Theologica*, First Part, Question 2, Article 3, translated by The Fathers of the English Dominican Province, second and revised edition (1920), http://www.domcentral.org/summa/a4/summa-Iq2a3.pdf.
76. Calvin, *Institutes*, 51.
77. Isaac Newton, "General Scholium" from *The Mathematical Principles of Natural Philosophy* [1729], *The Newton Project*, June 2009, https://www.newtonproject.ox.ac.uk/view/texts/normalized/NATP00056; also see Vincent J. Torley, "Newton on Intelligent Design," *Uncommon Descent*, March 14, 2013, https://uncommondescent.com/intelligent-design/newton-on-intelligent-design/.
78. Isaac Newton, "Draft of the 'Hypothesis Concerning Light and Colors,'" *The Newton Project*, June 2011, https://www.newtonproject.ox.ac.uk/view/texts/normalized/NATP00121.
79. John Ray, *The Wisdom of God Manifested in the Works of Creation* (Aberdeen, Scotland: J. Boyle, 1777), https://archive.org/details/b32999367/page/36/mode/2up, 35.
80. Richard Blackmore, *Creation. A Philosophical Poem. Demonstrating the Existence and Providence of a God. In Seven Books* (London: J. Tonson, 1715), https://archive.org/details/bim_eighteenth-century_creation-a-philosophica_blackmore-richard-sir_1715/page/n43/mode/2up, xliii.
81. Calvin, *Institutes*, 51.
82. Joseph Butler, *Analogy of Religion, in The Works of Bishop Butler*, ed. David E. White (Rochester, NY: University of Rochester Press, 2006), 299.
83. François de Salignac de La Mothe Fénelon, *A Demonstration of the Existence and Attributes of God* (London: W. Taylor, 1720), https://archive.org/details/bim_eighteenth-century_a-demonstration-of-the-e_fnelon-franois-de-sal_1720/page/4/mode/2up, 5.
84. Francis Hutcheson, *System of Moral Philosophy* (London: R. and A. Poulis, 1755), https://archive.org/details/systemmoralphilo01hutc/page/n5/mode/2up, I:35.
85. Samuel Clark[e], *A Demonstration of the Being and Attributes of God*, 2nd ed. (London: James Knapton, 1706), 177–178, https://archive.org/details/bim_eighteenth-century_a-demonstration-of-the-b_clarke-samuel_1706/.
86. Clark[e], *A Demonstration of the Being and Attributes of God*, 178.
87. Clark[e], *A Demonstration of the Being and Attributes of God*, 179.
88. Clark[e], *A Demonstration of the Being and Attributes of God*, 179–180, emphasis in the original.
89. Witherspoon, *Lectures on Moral Philosophy*, 96.
90. Wilson, *Lectures on Law*, I: 506.
91. Wilson, *Lectures on Law*, I: 504.
92. Benjamin Franklin, "Articles of Belief and Acts of Religion," November 20, 1728, *National Archives: Founders Online*, https://founders.archives.gov/documents/Franklin/01-01-02-0032.
93. Franklin, "Articles of Belief and Acts of Religion," note 7 and accompanying text.
94. Thomas Jefferson to John Adams, April 11, 1823, *National Archives: Founders Online*, https://founders.archives.gov/documents/Jefferson/03-19-02-0400.
95. Thomas Paine, *The Age of Reason*, part 1 (1793), *Thomas Paine Historical Association*, https://www.thomaspaine.org/writings/1793/the-age-of-reason-part-i.

96. Clip of Heidi Przybyla on *MSNBC*, posted by Erick Erickson (@EWErickson), *X*, February 23, 2024, 9:13 a.m., https://x.com/EWErickson/status/1761046517412937977.
97. Alexander Hall, "Kaine Sparks Backlash After Calling Declaration of Independence's God-Given Rights 'Extremely Troubling,'" *FoxNews.com*, September 4, 2025, https://www.foxnews.com/media/kaine-sparks-backlash-after-calling-declaration-independences-god-given-rights-extremely-troubling.
98. West, *How Americans View the American Founding*, 10.
99. Witherspoon, *Lectures on Moral Philosophy*, 111.
100. Francis Hutcheson, *An Inquiry into the Original of Our Ideas of Beauty and Virtue in Two Treatises*, rev. ed., ed. Wolfgang Leidhold (Indianapolis, IN: Liberty Fund, 2008), 186–187.
101. Hutcheson, *An Inquiry*, 187.
102. Wilson, *Law Lectures*, I: 534.
103. Wilson, *Law Lectures*, I: 638.
104. Witherspoon, *Lectures on Moral Philosophy*, 111.
105. "The Virginia Declaration of Rights" [1776], *National Archives*, https://www.archives.gov/founding-docs/virginia-declaration-of-rights, Section 16.
106. Hutcheson, *An Inquiry*, 188.
107. Witherspoon, *Lectures on Moral Philosophy*, 123. Also see Thomas Reid, *Essays on the Active Powers of Man* (1788), in *The Works of Thomas Reid*, 7th ed. (Edinburgh: Maclachlan and Stewart, 1872), II:658: "The natural right of liberty implies a right to such innocent labour as a man chooses, and to the fruit of that labour. To hinder another man's innocent labour, or to deprive him of the fruit of it, is an injustice of the same kind, and has the same effect, as to put him in fetters or in prison, and is equally a just object of resentment."
108. Thomas Jefferson, "First Inaugural Address" (US Capitol, Washington, DC, March 4, 1801), *National Archives: Founders Online*, https://founders.archives.gov/documents/Jefferson/01-33-02-0116-0004.
109. Simeon Howard, "A Sermon Preached to the Ancient and Honorable Artillery Company in Boston" [1773], *American Political Writing During the Founding Era, 1760–1805*, eds. Charles S. Hyneman and Donald S. Lutz (Indianapolis, IN: Liberty Press, 1983), I: 187.
110. Nathaniel Niles, "Two Discourses on Liberty" [1774], *American Political Writing during the Founding Era*, I:270.
111. Anonymous, "Rudiments of Law and Government Deduced from the Law of Nature" [1783], *American Political Writing during the Founding Era*, I: 575
112. "The Virginia Declaration of Rights," Section 15.
113. George Washington, "First Annual Message to Congress" (Joint Session of Congress, Federal Hall, New York City, January 8, 1790), https://millercenter.org/the-presidency/presidential-speeches/january-8-1790-first-annual-message-congress.
114. "Constitution of Massachusetts" [1780], Article III, *Consource*, https://www.consource.org/document/constitution-of-massachusetts-1780-10-25/.
115. Howard, "A Sermon," I: 187.

116. George Washington, "Farewell Address," *American Daily Advertiser*, September 19, 1796, *National Archives: Founders Online*, https://founders.archives.gov/documents/Washington/05-20-02-0440-0002.
117. Witherspoon, *Lectures on Moral Philosophy*, 159.
118. Benjamin Franklin to the Abbés Chalet and Arnaud, April 17, 1787, *The Works of Banjamin Franklin, Vol. XI, Letters and Miscellaneous Writings, 1784–1788*, ed. John Bigelow (New York: G. P. Putnam's Sons, 1904), vol. XI, https://oll.libertyfund.org/titles/franklin-the-works-of-benjamin-franklin-vol-xi-letters-and-misc-writings-1784–1788.
119. Personal communication to the author.
120. James Wilson, "Consideration on the Nature and Extent of the Legislative Authority of the British Parliament, 1774," *Collected Works*, I: 4.
121. Jaffa, *A New Birth of Freedom*, 106.

CHAPTER 3: A SECOND AMERICAN REVOLUTION

1. Alexander H. Stephens, "Cornerstone Speech" (Athenaeum, Savannah, GA, March 21, 1861), *American Battlefield Trust*, https://www.battlefields.org/learn/primary-sources/cornerstone-speech. All subsequent quotations from Stephens's speech come from this source.
2. For a more detailed discussion of key Founders and slavery, see Mark David Hall, *Proclaim Liberty Throughout All the Land: How Christianity Has Advanced Freedom and Equality for All Americans* (New York: Fidelis Books, 2023), Kindle, chap. 3.
3. Hall, *Proclaim Liberty Throughout All the Land*, 68.
4. Benjamin Franklin et al., "An Address to the Public from the Pennsylvania Society for Promoting the Abolition of Slavery, and the Relief of Free Negroes Unlawfully Held in Bondage," November 9, 1789, *The Works of Benjamin Franklin, Vol. XII, Letters and Misc. Writings 1788–1790, Supplement, Indexes*, ed. John Bigelow (New York: G. P. Putnam's Sons, 1904), https://oll.libertyfund.org/titles/franklin-the-works-of-benjamin-franklin-vol-xii-letters-and-misc-writings-1788–1790-supplement-indexes#lf1438-12_head_070.
5. Benjamin Franklin, President of the Pennsylvania Society for the Abolition of Slavery, "Petition from the Pennsylvania Society for the Abolition of Society," February 3, 1790, *USHistory.org*, https://www.ushistory.org/documents/antislavery.htm.
6. Hall, *Proclaim Liberty Throughout All the Land*, 67.
7. West, *The Politics of Revelation and Reason*, 53–56.
8. John Jay to R. Lushington, March 15, 1786, *The Correspondence and Public Papers of John Jay, Vol. 3 (1782–1793)*, ed. Henry P. Johnston, (New York: G. P. Putnam's Sons, 1890–1893), https://oll.libertyfund.org/titles/johnston-the-correspondence-and-public-papers-of-john-jay-vol-3-1782–1793.
9. James Madison, *Notes of Debates in the Federal Convention of 1787 Reported by James Madison* (New York: W. W. Norton, 1987), 77.
10. Thomas Jefferson, *Notes on the State of Virginia* [1787], ed. William Peden (New York: W.W. Norton, 1972), 163.
11. Thomas G. West, *Vindicating the Founders: Race, Sex, Class, and Justice in the Origins of America* (Lanham, MD: Rowman and Littlefield, 1997), 10–11.

12. West, *Vindicating the Founders*, 11.
13. "The Northwest Ordinance (1787)," *National Constitution Center*, https://constitutioncenter.org/the-constitution/historic-document-library/detail/the-northwest-ordinance. Section 6 of the Ordinance did allow servitude as a punishment for a crime, and it also provided for the return of fugitive slaves.
14. Van Gosse, *The First Reconstruction: Black Politics in America from the Revolution to the Civil War* (Chapel Hill, NC: University of North Carolina Press, 2021), 164–165.
15. "Articles of Confederation" [1777], Article IV, *National Archives*, https://www.archives.gov/milestone-documents/articles-of-confederation.
16. Gosse, *The First Reconstruction*, 34.
17. Gosse, *The First Reconstruction*, 6.
18. Gosse, *The First Reconstruction*, 169.
19. "The Cotton Gin: A Game-Changing Social and Economic Invention," *National Constitution Center*, March 14, 2024, https://constitutioncenter.org/blog/the-cotton-gin-a-game-changing-social-and-economic-invention; Hall, *Proclaim Liberty Throughout All the Land*, 84.
20. Henry Home, *Lord Kames, Sketches of the History of Man, Considerably Enlarged by the Last Additions and Corrections of the Author*, Book I, ed. James A. Harris (Indianapolis, IN: Liberty Fund, 2007), 46–47.
21. Kames, *Sketches of the History of Man*, 47.
22. Kames, *Sketches of the History of Man*, 47.
23. Samuel Stanhope Smith, *An Essay on the Causes of the Variety of Complexion and Figure in the Human Species* [Philadelphia, PA, 1787] (London: John Stockdale, 1789), 5.
24. Smith, *An Essay on the Causes of the Variety of Complexion*, 113.
25. Smith, *An Essay on the Causes of the Variety of Complexion*, 113–114.
26. Samuel Stanhope Smith, *An Essay on the Causes of the Variety of Complexion and Figure in the Human Species*, 2nd ed. (New Brunswick, NJ: J. Simpson and Co., 1810), 268–269.
27. Smith, *An Essay on the Causes of the Variety of Complexion* (1810), 269–270
28. Smith, *An Essay on the Causes of the Variety of Complexion* (1810), 269.
29. Samuel Stanhope Smith, *The Lectures, Corrected and Improved, Which Have Been Delivered for a Series of Years in the College of New Jersey; on the Subjects of Moral and Political Philosophy* (Trenton, NJ: Daniel Fenton, 1812), II: 176–177.
30. Quoted by Henry S. Patterson, "Memoir—Notice of the Life and Scientist Labors of the Late Samuel Geo. Morton, MD," in J. C. Nott and Geo. R. Gliddon, *Types of Mankind* (Philadelphia, PA: Lippincott, Grambo & Co., 1854), l.
31. Quoted by Patterson, "Memoir," li, emphasis in original.
32. Louis Agassiz, "Sketch of the Natural Province of the Animal World and Their Relation to the Different Types of Man," in Josiah Clark Nott and George Robins Gliddon, *Types of Mankind* (Philadelphia, PA: J. B. Lippincott, 1854), lxxv-lxxvi.
33. Agassiz, "Sketch," lxxvi.
34. Agassiz, "Sketch," lxxv.
35. Agassiz, "Sketch," lxxiv-lxxv.

36. Agassiz, "Sketch," lxxv.
37. J. C. Nott, "Introduction," in Nott and Gliddon, *Types of Mankind*, 56.
38. Nott, "Introduction," 60.
39. G. K. Chesterton, "The Future of Democracy," in *What I Saw in America* (London: Hodder and Stoughton, 1922), chap. 19, https://www.gutenberg.org /ebooks/27250, emphasis in original. Jefferson Davis was the president of the Confederacy. To be clear, Chesterton in these comments was being critical of the claims of scientific racism.
40. Frederick Douglass, "The Claims of the Negro, Ethnologically Considered" (commencement address, Literary Societies of Western Reserve College, Hudson, OH, July 12, 1854), https://tile.loc.gov/storage-services/service/rbc/rbaapc /07900/07900.pdf, 4.
41. Douglass, "The Claims of the Negro," 5.
42. Douglass, "The Claims of the Negro," 4.
43. Moncure Daniel Conway, *Autobiography: Memories and Experiences of Moncure Daniel Conway* (Boston, MA: Houghton, Mifflin and Company, 1904), I: 89.
44. Conway, *Autobiography*, I: 89.
45. Conway, *Autobiography*, I: 90.

CHAPTER 4: THE TRIUMPH OF SCIENTOCRACY

1. Daniel Dennett, *Darwin's Dangerous Idea: Evolution and the Meanings of Life* (New York: Touchstone, 1995), 18.
2. Charles Darwin, *On the Origin of Species by Means of Natural Selection*, 1st ed. (London: John Murray, 1859), 484.
3. Charles Darwin, *The Autobiography of Charles Darwin, 1809–1882, with Original Omissions Restored*, ed. Nora Barlow (New York: Norton, 1969), 87.
4. Darwin, *On the Origin of Species*, 490.
5. Hugh Elliot, *Modern Science and Materialism* (London: Longmans, Green, and Co., 1927), 138.
6. Richard Dawkins, *The Blind Watchmaker: Why the Evidence of Evolution Reveals a Universe Without Design* (New York: W. W. Norton, 1996), 6.
7. Edward O. Wilson, *Consilience: The Unity of Knowledge* (New York: Alfred Knopf, 1998), 241.
8. David Barash, "God, Darwin, and My Biology Class," *New York Times*, September 27, 2014, www.nytimes.com/2014/09/28/opinion/sunday/god-darwin -and-my-college-biology-class.html.
9. James H. Leuba, *The Belief in God and Immortality: A Psychological, Anthropological and Statistical Study* (Boston, MA: Sherman, French, and Company, 1916), 254–255.
10. Leuba, *The Belief in God and Immortality*, 261.
11. Leuba, *The Belief in God and Immortality*, 268.
12. John G. West, *Darwin's Corrosive Idea: The Impact of Evolution on Attitudes about Faith, Ethics, & Human Uniqueness* (Seattle: Discovery Institute, 2016), 2, 7.
13. West, *Darwin's Corrosive Idea*, 10.
14. John Polkinghorne, Quarks, *Chaos, and Christianity*, rev. ed. (New York: Crossroad, 2006), 113.

15. Kenneth R. Miller, *Finding Darwin's God: A Scientist's Search for Common Ground Between God and Evolution* (New York: HarperCollins, 1999), 272; see also 244.
16. George V. Coyne, S. J., "The Dance of the Fertile Universe," accessed January 8, 2026, https://web.archive.org/web/20051104052227/http://www.aei.org/docLib/20051027_HandoutCoyne.pdf, 7.
17. Karl Giberson, *Saving Darwin: How to Be a Christian and Believe in Evolution* (New York: HarperOne, 2008), 12.
18. Francis S. Collins, *The Language of God: A Scientist Presents Evidence for Belief* (New York: Free Press, 2006), 205.
19. See John G. West, "Nothing New Under the Sun: Theistic Evolution, the Early Church, and the Return of Gnosticism, Part 1," in Jay Richards, ed., *God and Evolution: Protestants, Catholics, and Jews Explore Darwin's Challenge to Faith* (Seattle: Discovery Institute Press, 2010); William A. Dembski, Wayne J. Downs, and Father Justin B. A. Frederick, eds., *The Patristic Understanding of Creation: An Anthology of Writings from the Church Fathers on Creation and Design* (Riesel, TX: Erasmus Press, 2008).
20. Thomas Jefferson to Roger C. Weightman, June 24, 1826, "Declaring Independence: Drafting the Documents," *Library of Congress*, https://www.loc.gov/exhibits/declara/rcwltr.html.
21. See "The Somerset v. Stewart Case," *English Heritage*, accessed December 17, 2025, https://www.english-heritage.org.uk/visit/places/kenwood/history-stories-kenwood/somerset-case/; and Richard Sheposh, "1807, Act on the Abolition of the Slave Trade in the British Empire," *EBSCO Knowledge Advantage*, 2023, https://www.ebsco.com/research-starters/law/1807-act-abolition-slave-trade-british-empire.
22. Natasha L. Henry, "Slavery Abolition Act," *Britannica*, accessed December 17, 2025, https://www.britannica.com/topic/Slavery-Abolition-Act.
23. Stephen Jay Gould, *Ontogeny and Phylogeny* (Cambridge, MA: Belknap Press/Harvard, 1977), 127.
24. Charles Darwin, *The Descent of Man, and Selection in Relation to Sex* [1871] (Princeton, NJ: Princeton UP, 1981), I: 109–110.
25. Darwin, *The Descent of Man*, I: 201. For more on Darwinian racism, see John G. West, *Darwin Day in America: How Our Politics and Culture Have Been Dehumanized in the Name of Science*, expanded paperback edition (Wilmington, DE: ISI Books, 2015), 144–150 and accompanying notes.
26. Richard Weikart, *From Darwin to Hitler: Evolutionary Ethics, Eugenics, and Racism in Germany* (New York: Palgrave Macmillan, 2004), 106–107.
27. Charles Davenport [1866–1944], "Scientific Cooperation with Nature: Eugenics," undated, typescript in Charles Davenport Papers, Collection B D27, American Philosophical Society, Philadelphia, 2.
28. See Nancy J. Parezo and Don D. Fowler, *Anthropology Goes to the Fair: The 1904 Louisiana Purchase Exposition* (Lincoln, NE: Nebraska UP, 2007); and *Human Zoos: America's Forgotten History of Scientific Racism,* written and directed by John G. West, Discovery Institute, 2018, https://youtu.be/nY6Zrol5QEk. More generally, see Pascal Blanchard et al., *Human Zoos: Science and Spectacle in the Age of Colonial Empires*, trans. Teresa Bridgeman (Liverpool, UK: Liverpool UP, 2008).
29. W. J. McGee, "Anthropology at the Louisiana Purchase Exposition," *Science* 22, no. 573 (December 22, 1905): 814.

30. "Pygmies May Be the Missing Link," *St. Louis Republic*, July 10, 1904, 9.
31. See *Human Zoos: America's Forgotten History of Scientific Racism*; Pamela Newkirk, *Spectacle: The Astonishing Life of Ota Benga* (New York: Amistad, 2015); and Phillips Verner Bradford and Harvey Blume, *Ota Benga: The Pygmy in the Zoo* (New York: Delta, 1992).
32. "Negro Clergy Protest," *New York Daily Tribune*, September 11, 1906, 8. According to today's terminology, Ota Benga wasn't displayed with a "monkey." He was displayed with an ape (an orangutan is an ape, and so is a chimpanzee). But in the early 1900s, the term monkey was often loosely applied to apes as well as to those we would consider monkeys today.
33. "Negro Ministers Act to Free the Pygmy," *The New York Times*, September 11, 1906, https://humanzoos.org/wp-content/uploads/sites/18/2018/01/ministersactnyt091106.pdf
34. "Topics of the Times: Send Him Back to the Woods," *The New York Times*, September 11, 1906, https://humanzoos.org/wp-content/uploads/sites/18/2018/01/sendhimnyt091106.pdf.
35. Charles Francis Adams, Jr., *"'Tis Sixty Years Since": An Address* (US Senate, Washington, DC, 1913), 9.
36. The publication's title page states: "Presented by Mr. Clapp for Mr. Tillman."
37. John G. West, "Honored by Statue, Democratic South Carolina Senator Said Some Blacks 'Near Akin to Monkey,'" *Science & Culture Today*, July 16, 2021, https://scienceandculture.com/2021/07/honored-by-statue-democratic-south-carolina-senator-said-some-blacks-near-akin-to-monkey-2/.
38. Edward M. East, *Mankind at the Crossroads* (New York: Charles Scribner's Sons, 1923), 137–138. In a later book, however, East acknowledged that "it is of no importance whether the negro or the white man is more closely related to the apes." Edward M. East, *Heredity and Human Affairs* (New York: Charles Scribner's Sons, 1927), 189.
39. Charles Davenport [1866–1944], "A Biologist's View of the Negro Problem," undated, handwritten manuscript in Charles Davenport Papers, Collection B D27, American Philosophical Society, Philadelphia, 3.
40. Charles Davenport, "Protection of the National Germ Plasm," December 31, 1920, in Charles Davenport Papers, Collection B D27, American Philosophical Society, Philadelphia, 1.
41. Davenport, "Scientific Cooperation with Nature," 2; East, *Heredity and Human Affairs*, 194–195; East, *Mankind at the Crossroads*, 134–136.
42. Davenport [1866–1944], "Do Races Differ in Mental Capacity?," undated, in Charles Davenport Papers, Collection B D27, American Philosophical Society, Philadelphia, [hand pagination], 10, also 3–4.
43. West, *Darwin Day in America*, 134–135.
44. See Charlotte Hunt-Grubbe, "The Elementary DNA of Dr. Watson," *The Sunday Times*, October 14, 2007, https://www.thetimes.co.uk/article/the-elementary-dna-of-dr-watson-gllb6w2vpdr; and James D. Watson, *Avoid Boring People: Lessons from a Life in Science* (New York: Alfred Knopf, 2007), 326.
45. Meilan Solly, "DNA Pioneer James Watson Loses Honorary Titles Over Racist Comments," *Smithsonian*, January 15, 2019, https://www.smithsonianmag.com/smart-news/dna-pioneer-james-watson-loses-honorary-titles-over-racist-comments-180971266/.

46. "Madison Grant and the American Nation," *Radix Journal*, October 8, 2016, https://radixjournal.altright.com/2016/10/2016-10-6-madison-grant-and-the-american-nation/.
47. Brian Resnick, "Psychologists Surveyed Hundreds of Alt-Right Supporters. The Results Are Unsettling," *Vox*, August 12, 2018, https://www.vox.com/science-and-health/2017/8/15/16144070/psychology-alt-right-unite-the-right.
48. Mencius Moldbug [Curtis Yarvin], "A Gentle Introduction to Unqualified Reservations, Chapter 7: The War of Secession," *Unqualified Reservations*, March 5, 2009, https://www.unqualified-reservations.org/2009/03/gentle-introduction-to-unqualified/.
49. Quoted in David Klinghoffer, "James von Brunn, Evolutionist," *Kingdom of Priests*, June 2009, https://www.beliefnet.com/columnists/kingdomofpriests/2009/06/james-von-brunn-evolutionist.html.
50. Quoted in John G. West, "How Science Fueled the White Supremacist Mass Murderer in Buffalo, NY," *Science & Culture Today*, May 16, 2022, https://scienceandculture.com/2022/05/how-science-fueled-the-white-supremacist-mass-murderer-in-buffalo-ny/.
51. Darwin, *Descent of Man*, I: 35.
52. Darwin, *Descent of Man*, I: 46.
53. Darwin, *Descent of Man*, I: 49–50.
54. Darwin, *Descent of Man*, I: 51.
55. Darwin, *Descent of Man*, I: 56.
56. Paul Barrett et. al., *Charles Darwin's Notebooks, 1836–1844* (New York: Cornell UP, 1987), 165.
57. Barrett, *Charles Darwin's Notebooks*, 613–614.
58. Darwin, *Descent of Man*, I: 91.
59. Barrett, *Charles Darwin's Notebooks*, 608, emphasis in original.
60. Barrett, *Charles Darwin's Notebooks*, 608, emphasis in original.
61. Darwin, *Descent of Man*, I: 65–67.
62. Barrett, *Charles Darwin's Notebooks*, 189.
63. Barrett, *Charles Darwin's Notebooks*, 222–223.
64. East, *Heredity and Human Affairs*, 29.
65. Quoted in Maggie Fox, "Fly Gene Map May Have Many Uses, Scientists Say," *Reuters*, March 23, 2000, http://dailynews.yahoo.com/h/nm/20000323/sc/fly_uses_2.html.
66. Patricia Reaney, "Are You Man or Mouse? Check Your Genes… ," *Reuters*, December 4, 2002, http://story.news.yahoo.com/news?tmpl=story2&cid=570&u=/nm/20021204/.
67. Derek E. Wilman et al., "Implications of Natural Selection in Shaping 99.4% Nonsynonymous DNA Identity Between Humans and Chimpanzees: Enlarging Genus Homo," *Proceedings of the National Academy of Sciences* 100, no. 12 (June 10, 2003): 7181. Goodman is identified as the contributor of this article to *Proceedings*.
68. John Derbyshire, "What's So Scary about Evolution?—for Both Right and Left, a Lot," *Taki's Magazine*, May 19, 2008, http://www.johnderbyshire.com/Opinions/HumanSciences/darwin.html, emphasis in original.

69. Quoted in Johann Hari, "Peter Singer—An Interview," originally run in *The Independent*, January 7, 2004, https://web.archive.org/web/20060317041348/http://www.johannhari.com/archive/article.php?id=410.
70. William Provine, abstract for "Evolution: Free Will and Punishment and Meaning in Life" (lecture, Second Annual Darwin Day Celebration, University of Tennessee, Knoxville, TN, February 12, 1998), posted at *Darwin Day Archives*, http://eeb.bio.utk.edu/darwin/DarwinDayProvineAddress.htm.
71. Robert Wright, *The Moral Animal: Evolutionary Psychology and Everyday Life* (New York: Vintage Books, 1995), 350. This is the paperback edition. The hardcover was originally published in 1994.
72. Wright, *The Moral Animal*, 37.
73. Wright, *The Moral Animal*, 37.
74. Wright, *The Moral Animal*, 88.
75. Maurice Parmelee, "Introduction," in Cesare Lombroso, *Crime: Its Causes and Remedies*, trans. Henry Horton (Montclair, NJ: Patterson Smith, 1968), xiv–xv; William Noyes, "The Criminal Type," *Journal of Social Science* 24 (April 1888): 32–34. For a discussion of Lombroso and Social Darwinism, see Mike Hawkins, *Social Darwinism in European and American Thought, 1860–1945* (Cambridge, UK: Cambridge UP, 1997), 74–80.
76. Noyes, "The Criminal Type," 34.
77. Lombroso, quoted by Parmelee in Lombroso, *Crime*, xviii.
78. Enrico Ferri, "The Positive School of Criminology," in *Criminology: A Book of Readings*, eds. Clyde Vedder, Samuel Koenig, and Robert Clark (New York: The Dryden Press, 1953), 137–138.
79. Steven Pinker, "Why They Kill Their Newborns," *The New York Times Magazine*, November 2, 1997, https://www.nytimes.com/1997/11/02/magazine/why-they-kill-their-newborns.html.
80. See West, *Darwin Day in America*, 325–333.
81. Jonathan Wells, *Icons of Evolution: Science or Myth?* (Washington, DC: Regnery, 2000), 87–101; Gould, *Ontogeny and Phylogeny*.
82. Testimony of Dr. James Neel, May 20, 1981, in *The Human Life Bill: Hearings Before the Subcommittee on Separation of Powers of the Committee on the Judiciary, United States Senate, Ninety-Seventh Congress, First Session, on S. 158, a Bill to Provide that Human Life Shall be Deemed to Exist from Conception, April 23, 24; May 20, 21; June 1, 10, 12 and 18. Serial No. J-97-16* (Washington, DC: US Government Printing Office, 1982), 77.
83. Carl Sagan and Ann Druyan, "Is It Possible to Be Pro-Life and Pro-Choice?" *Parade Magazine*, April 22, 1990, 6.
84. Christopher Hitchens, *God Is Not Great: How Religion Poisons Everything* (New York: Twelve, 2007), 221.
85. Jerry Coyne, "Should One Be Allowed to Euthanize Severely Deformed or Doomed Newborns?," *Why Evolution Is True*, July 13, 2017, https://whyevolutionistrue.com/2017/07/13/should-one-be-allowed-to-euthanize-severely-deformed-or-doomed-newborns/.
86. Wesley J. Smith, *The War on Humans* (Seattle: Discovery Institute Press, 2014).
87. Eric R. Pianka, "The Vanishing Book of Life on Earth," accessed January 8, 2026, http://www.zo.utexas.edu/courses/bio373/Vanishing.Book.pdf, 21.

88. Pianka, "Vanishing Book," 10.
89. Pianka, "Vanishing Book," 19.
90. Pianka, "Vanishing Book," 17; Jamie Mobley, "Doomsday: UT Prof Says Death Is Imminent," *Seguin Gazette-Enterprise*, February 27, 2010.
91. Christopher Manes, *Green Rage: Radical Environmentalism and the Unmaking of Civilization* (Boston: Little, Brown, 1990), 142.
92. James Lee, "The Discovery Channel MUST Broadcast to the World Their Commitment to Save the Planet and to Do the Following IMMEDIATELY," accessed January 8, 2026, https://web.archive.org/web/20101220024835/http://savetheplanetprotest.com/.
93. Quoted in Frederick Albert Lange, *History of Materialism*, trans. Ernest Chester Thomas (London: Kegan Paul, Trench, Trübner, & Co. Ltd., 1892), II: 312.
94. Stephen Jay Gould, *Ever Since Darwin: Reflections in Natural History* (New York: Norton, 1977), 13.
95. Darwin, *Descent of Man*, II: 362. Also see discussion in John G. West, *Darwin's Conservatives: The Misguided Quest* (Seattle: Discovery Institute Press, 2006), 19–32; and West, *Darwin Day in America*, 23–42.
96. John G. West, *How Americans View the American Founding* (Discovery Institute, 2026), 9, https://endowedbyourcreator.com/survey.
97. Wright, *The Moral Animal*, 146.
98. See West, *Darwin Day in America*, 271–290.
99. Christopher Ryan, quoted in Thomas Rogers, "'Sex at Dawn': Why Monogamy Goes Against Our Nature," *Salon*, June 27, 2010, https://www.salon.com/2010/06/27/sex_at_dawn_interview/. Also see Christopher Ryan and Cacilda Jetha, *Sex at Dawn: How We Mate, Why We Stray, and What It Means for Modern Relationships* (New York: Harper Perennial, 2011); Christopher Ryan and Calcida Jetha, "Open Marriage: We Don't Believe in Monogamy," *The Times*, July 24, 2010, https://www.thetimes.co.uk/article/open-marriage-we-dont-believe-in-monogamy-vz6lm77bfzc.
100. Friedrich Nietzsche, *On the Use and Abuse of History for Life* [1874], trans. Ian Johnston, rev. ed. (Arlington, VA: Richer Resources Publications, 2010), https://johnstoniatexts.x10host.com/nietzsche/historyhtml.html.
101. See Friedrich Nietzsche, *The Will to Power* [1901], ed. Walter Kaufmann (New York: Vintage Books, 1968), 512–513, 518–519; and Friedrich Nietzsche, *Thus Spake Zarathustra* [1883–1885], trans. Thomas Common (United Kingdom, 1909), https://www.gutenberg.org/files/1998/1998-h/1998-h.htm.
102. West, *How Americans View the American Founding*, 11.
103. Alex Nitzberg, "Mamdani Victory Speech Draws Concern as NYC Mayor-Elect Vows 'No Problem Too Large for Government to Solve,'" *FoxNews.com*, November 5, 2025, https://www.foxnews.com/politics/mamdani-victory-speech-draws-concern-nyc-mayor-elect-vows-no-problem-too-large-government-solve. Although significant, the number of Americans who explicitly embrace Mamdani's expansive view of government is still a minority, only about 26 percent of Americans as a whole. See West, *How Americans View the American Founding*, 11.
104. Henry David Thoreau, *On the Duty of Civil Disobedience* [1849], https://www.gutenberg.org/cache/epub/71/pg71.txt.

105. Thoreau, *Civil Disobedience*, emphasis in original.
106. John Burgess, *Political Science and Comparative Constitutional Law* (New York: Baker and Taylor, 1890), I: 85.
107. "Apotheosis," *Etymonline*, https://www.etymonline.com/word/apotheosis.
108. Charles Edward Merriam, *A History of American Political Theories* (New York: Macmillan, 1920), 310.
109. Merriam, *History of American Political Theories*, 332.
110. Carl Becker, *The Declaration of Independence: A Study in the History of Political Ideas* (New York: Harcourt, Brace and Company, 1922), 274–275.
111. Westel Woodbury Willoughby, *An Examination of the Nature of the State: A Study in Political Philosophy* (New York: Macmillan, 1896), 107.
112. Merriam, *History of American Political Theories*, 313.
113. Merriam, *History of American Political Theories*, 314.
114. Willoughby, *An Examination of the Nature of the State*, 338.
115. Dennis John Mahoney, "A New Political Science for a World Made Wholly New: The Doctrine of Progress and the Emergence of American Political Science" (PhD diss., Claremont Graduate School, 1984), 25–45.
116. Woodrow Wilson, *Constitutional Government in the United States* (New York: Columbia UP, 1911), 55.
117. Woodrow Wilson, *The New Freedom* (Garden City, NY: Doubleday, Page, and Co., 1921), 45–47.
118. Wilson, *The New Freedom*, 47.
119. Wilson, *The New Freedom*, 48.
120. Robert Bannister, *Social Darwinism: Science and Myth in Anglo-American Social Thought*, with a new preface (Philadelphia: Temple University, 1988), 114.
121. West, *Darwin Day in America*, 105–113. Ironically, after left-wing reformers had stigmatized capitalism as "Social Darwinism," some on the right embraced a Darwinian justification of capitalism. But as I point out in another book, their analogizing from Darwinism to free enterprise was deeply flawed. The Darwinian process in nature is supposed to be blind to intelligence and the future. Random (i.e., non-guided) variations are in the driver's seat. By contrast, variations in the economy are drive by human beings exercising their intelligence and foresight. For a more detailed discussion of why Darwinism is a dead end as a justification for capitalism, see West, *Darwin Day in America*, 114–117.
122. Lester F. Ward, "Collective Telesis. Contributions to Social Philosophy. XII," *American Journal of Sociology 2*, no. 6 (May 1897): 821.
123. Lester F. Ward, *Dynamic Sociology, or Applied Social Science as Based upon Statical Sociology and the Less Complex Sciences* (New York: Appleton, 1883), II: 251–252.
124. "Eugenics in Politics," *The New York Times*, October 9, 1921, 93.
125. J. McKeen Cattell, "Homo Scientificus Americanus," *Science* 17, no. 432 (April 10, 1903): 569.
126. Charles W. Eliot, "The Fruits, Prospects and Lessons of Recent Biological Science," *Science* 42, no. 1096 (December 31, 1915): 926.
127. Darwin, *Descent of Man*, I: 168.
128. Daniel J. Kevles, *In the Name of Eugenics: Genetics and the Uses of Human Heredity* (Cambridge, MA: Harvard UP, 1995), xiii.

129. West, *Darwin Day in America*, 161.

130. West, *Darwin Day in America*, 135–150. A full critique of the eugenics movement is beyond the scope of this book. But it is worth noting that eugenicists based their arguments on arguable assumptions and presented the public with a false set of choices about social policy. First, many dysfunctional behaviors are not the result of heredity, so curtailing reproduction will not eliminate them. Second, the forced curtailment of reproduction is not the only way to address the growth in dysfunctional populations. The strengthening of character-building institutions such as churches and youth programs like scouting is another approach. Third, eugenicists tended to present an inaccurate picture of the nation being swamped by severely mentally disabled individuals currently housed in institutions. Yet those sufficiently disabled to be permanently housed in an institution were not bearing many children, even assuming that most of their disabilities were hereditary, which is a highly questionable assumption.

131. East, *Heredity and Human Affairs*, 237.

132. Edwin Conklin, "Value of Negative Eugenics," *Journal of Heredity* 6, no. 12 (December 1915): 539–540.

133. Alfred Edward Wiggam, "Does Heredity or Environment Make Men?" in Horatio Hackett Newman, *Evolution, Genetics, and Eugenics*, 3rd ed. (Chicago: University of Chicago Press, 1932), 505.

134. James Wilson, "Presidential Address," *American Breeders Magazine* 4, no. 1 (First Quarter, 1913): 56.

135. Mark H. Haller, *Eugenics: Hereditarian Attitudes in American Thought* (New Brunswick, NJ: Rutgers UP, 1963), 141.

136. "Remembering the 'Forgotten Victims' of Nazi 'Euthanasia' Murders," *Deutsche Welle*, January 26, 2017, https://www.dw.com/en/remembering-the-forgotten-victims-of-nazi-euthanasia-murders/a-37286088; Leo Alexander, "Medical Science Under Dictatorship," *New England Journal of Medicine* 241, no. 2 (July 14, 1949): 39–47; Michael Burleigh, *Death and Deliverance: "Euthanasia" in Germany 1900–1945* (Cambridge, MA: Cambridge UP, 1994).

Chapter 5: Back to the Future

1. For more information about the life and work of Asher Durand, see John Durand, *The Life and Times of A. B. Durand* (New York: Charles Scribner's Sons, 1894); "Declaration of Independence" [the John Trumbull painting], *Architect of the Capitol*, https://www.aoc.gov/explore-capitol-campus/art/declaration-independence; Kevin J. Avery, "Asher Brown Durand (1796–1886)," *The Metropolitan Museum of Art*, October 1, 2009, https://www.metmuseum.org/essays/asher-brown-durand-1796–1886.
2. Durand, *Life and Times*, 4.
3. Asher Durand, quoted in Durand, *Life and Times*, 19.
4. Asher Durand, quoted in Durand, *Life and Times*, 20.
5. Durand, *Life and Times*, 3.
6. Durand, *Life and Times*, 7–8.
7. Durand, *Life and Times*, 24–25.
8. Durand, *Life and Times*, 32–33.
9. Durand, *Life and Times*, 30.

10. Durand, *Life and Times*, 31.
11. Durand, *Life and Times*, 25–26.
12. Asher Durand, "Letter IX," in Linda S. Ferber, ed., *Kindred Spirits: Asher B. Durand and the American Landscape* (London: Brooklyn Museum/D. Giles Limited, 2007), 252.
13. Durand, "Letter VIII," in Ferber, *Kindred Spirits*, 248.
14. Durand, "Letter II," in Ferber, *Kindred Spirits*, 235.
15. Charles Darwin, *The Autobiography of Charles Darwin and Selected Letters*, ed. Francis Darwin (New York: Dover Publications, 1958), 65.
16. Darwin, *Autobiography*, 65.
17. "The old argument from design in Nature... which formerly seemed to me so conclusive, fails, now that the law of natural selection has been discovered." Darwin, *Autobiography*, 63.
18. Darwin, *Autobiography*, 53–54.
19. Durand, *Life and Times*, 209.
20. Stephen C. Meyer, "A Scopes Trial for the '90s," *The Wall Street Journal*, December 6, 1993, https://www.discovery.org/1993/12/danger-indoctrination/.
21. See Edward Larson, *Summer for the Gods: The Scopes Trial and America's Continuing Debate over Science and Religion* (New York: Basic Books, 1997); Carol Iannone, "The Truth about Inherit the Wind," *First Things*, February 1997, https://firstthings.com/002-the-truth-about-inherit-the-wind-36/; and Marvin Olasky and John Perry, *Monkey Business: The True Story of the Scopes Trial* (Nashville, TN: Broadman and Holman, 2005).
22. Richard Dawkins, *The Blind Watchmaker: Why the Evidence of Evolution Reveals a Universe Without Design* (New York: W.W. Norton, 1996), 6.
23. Richard Dawkins, *River Out of Eden: A Darwinian View of Life* (New York: Basic Books, 1995), 133.
24. Justin Brierley, *The Surprising Rebirth of Belief in God: Why New Atheism Grew Old and Secular Thinkers Are Considering Christianity Again* (Carol Stream, IL: Tyndale Elevate, 2023).
25. Stephen C. Meyer, *Return of the God Hypothesis: Three Scientific Discoveries that Reveal the Mind Behind the Universe* (New York: HarperOne, 2021).
26. For a good account, see Jean-Pierre Luminet, *The Big Bang Revolutionaries: The Untold Story of Three Scientists Who Reenchanted Cosmology* (Seattle: Discovery Institute Press, 2024).
27. Meyer, *Return of the God Hypothesis*, 69–129; "Big Bang: Something from Nothing?," *Science Uprising*, episode 7, Discovery Institute, September 15, 2021, video, 9:39, https://scienceuprising.com/bang/.
28. Malcolm W. Browne, "Clues to Universe Origin Expected," *The New York Times*, March 12, 1978, https://www.nytimes.com/1978/03/12/archives/clues-to-universe-origin-expected-the-making-of-the-universe.html.
29. "Big Bang: Something from Nothing?" at 05:33.
30. "Big Bang: Something from Nothing?" at 03:25.
31. "Big Bang: Something from Nothing?" at 07:36.
32. See Meyer, *Return of the God Hypothesis*, especially 348–406; and Bruce Gordon, Casey Luskin, and Brian Miller, "Dealing with Further Objections to 'Proof of

God in 3 Minutes,'" *Science & Culture Today*, October 17, 2025, https://scienceandculture.com/2025/10/dealing-with-further-objections-to-proof-of-god-in-3-minutes/.

33. Freeman Dyson, *Disturbing the Universe* (New York: Harper and Row, 1979), 250.
34. *Privileged Species*, Discovery Institute, 2015, video, 32:14, at 04:38, https://youtu.be/VoI2ms5UHWg?si=HDqhoxI0CLssRM5k.
35. This paragraph was adapted from my script for *Privileged Species*. See prior reference note. For documentation of fine-tuning parameters, see Jay W. Richards, "List of Fine-Tuning Parameters," *Discovery Institute*, https://www.discovery.org/m/securepdfs/2018/12/List-of-Fine-Tuning-Parameters-Jay-Richards.pdf; and Guillermo Gonzalez and Jay W. Richards, *The Privileged Planet: How Our Place in the Cosmos Is Designed for Discovery, 20th Anniversary Edition* (New York: Regnery, 2024).
36. Bonnie Azab Powell, "'Explore as Much as We Can': Noble Prize Winner Charles Townes on Evolution, Intelligent Design, and the Meaning of Life," *UCBerkeleyNews*, June 17, 2005, https://newsarchive.berkeley.edu/news/media/releases/2005/06/17_townes.shtml.
37. Sir Fred Hoyle, "The Universe: Past and Present Reflections," *Engineering and Science*, November 1981, 12.
38. Henry Quastler, *The Emergence of Biological Organization* (New Haven, CT: Yale UP,1964), 16.
39. See Stephen C. Meyer, *Darwin's Doubt: The Explosive Origin of Animal Life and the Case for Intelligent Design* (New York: HarperOne, 2013); "Mysterious Origins," *Science Uprising*, episode 9, Discovery Institute, November 17, 2021, video, 9:34, https://scienceuprising.com/fossils/; Günter Bechly, *The Fossil Record v. Darwin* (Seattle: Discovery Institute, 2021).
40. Transcript of ColdWater Media interview with Stephen Meyer, October 12, 2001.
41. Transcript of ColdWater Media interview with Meyer.
42. Endorsement by Brian Josephson, *Return of the God Hypothesis* [website], Discovery Institute, accessed January 8, 2026, https://returnofthegodhypothesis.com/book/endorsements/.
43. Thomas Jefferson to John Adams, April 11, 1823, *National Archives: Founders Online*, https://founders.archives.gov/documents/Jefferson/03-19-02-0400.
44. Casey Luskin, "Bombshell: New Research Overturns Claim that Humans and Chimps Differ by Only 1 Percent of DNA," *Science & Culture Today*, May 20, 2025, https://scienceandculture.com/2025/05/bombshell-new-research-overturns-claim-that-humans-and-chimps-differ-by-only-1-percent-of-dna/.
45. Luskin, "Bombshell."
46. Christine Webb, *The Arrogant Ape: The Myth of Human Exceptionalism and Why It Matters* (New York: Avery, 2025).
47. Webb, *The Arrogant Ape*, 1.
48. Philip Lieberman, "Why Human Speech Is Special," *The Scientist* (July 2018), https://www.the-scientist.com/features/why-human-speech-is-special--64351.
49. Terence W. Deacon, *The Symbolic Species: The Co-Evolution of Language and the Brain* (New York: W. W. Norton, 1997), 21–22.

50. Herbert Terrace, "Why Chimpanzees Can't Learn Language," *Psychology Today*, October 2, 2019, https://www.psychologytoday.com/us/blog/the-origin-words /201910/why-chimpanzees-cant-learn-language-1.
51. Victoria Wobber et al., "Differences in the Early Cognitive Development of Children and Great Apes," *Developmental Psychobiology* 56 (2013): 555, https://www.eva.mpg.de/documents/Wiley-Blackwell/Wobber_Differences _DevPsychobio_2014_1837160.pdf.
52. David Schultz, "Humans Can Outlearn Chimps Thanks to More Flexible Brain Genetics" *Science*, November 16, 2015, https://www.science.org/content/article /humans-can-outlearn-chimps-thanks-more-flexible-brain-genetics.
53. Charles Darwin, *The Descent of Man and Selection in Relation to Sex*, 2nd ed. (London: John Murray, 1877), 81.
54. "Build a Beaver Dam," *National Park Service*, accessed December 17, 2025, https://www.nps.gov/articles/buildabeaverdam.htm.
55. "Hoover Dam: Frequently Asked Questions and Answers—Hydropower at Hoover Dam," *US Bureau of Reclamation*, accessed December 17, 2025, https:// www.usbr.gov/lc/hooverdam/faqs/powerfaq.html; "Hoover Dam: Frequently Asked Questions and Answers—the Dam," *US Bureau of Reclamation*, accessed December 17, 2025, https://www.usbr.gov/lc/hooverdam/faqs/damfaqs.html.
56. "Notre-Dame de Paris," *Britannica*, December 8, 2025, https://www.britannica .com/topic/Notre-Dame-de-Paris.
57. G. K. Chesterton, *The Everlasting Man* (London: Hodder and Stoughton, 1925), 41.
58. The following section is based on my script for the documentary *Fire-Maker: How Humans Were Designed to Harness Fire and Transform Our Planet*, written and directed by John G. West, Discovery Institute, 2016, https://youtu.be /an98jVCyApo?si=azlcUSOlj2mgrkij.=; John G. West, "Fire-Maker: How Humans Were Designed to Harness Fire and Transform Our Planet," Final Script, November 20, 2015. For documentation, see Michael Denton, *Fire -Maker: How Humans Were Designed to Harness Fire and Transform Our Planet* (Seattle: Discovery Institute Press, 2016).
59. "Fire-Maker," Final Script, 5.
60. *Fire-Maker* (documentary) at 10:13.
61. James Kalat, *Introduction to Psychology*, 4th ed. (Pacific Grove, CA: Brooks/Cole, 1996), 8.
62. "INR5: Jerry Coyne, 'You Don't Have Free Will" (presentation, "Imagine No Religion 5" Conference, Vancouver, Canada, June 2015), posted at *YouTube*, July 7, 2015, video, 51:52, at 01:35, https://youtu.be/Ca7i-D4ddaw?si =8bMw0M88Za-Jugql.
63. Francis Crick, *The Astonishing Hypothesis: The Scientific Search for the Soul* (New York: Charles Scribner's Sons, 1994), 3.
64. Michael Egnor, "Neuroscience and Dualism," in Angus J. Menuge, Brian R. Krouse, and Robert J. Marks, *Minding the Brain: Models of the Mind, Information, and Empirical Science* (Seattle: Discovery Institute Press, 2023), 257, emphasis in original.
65. Quoted in Egnor, "Neuroscience and Dualism," 257.
66. Egnor, "Neuroscience and Dualism," 257.

67. Egnor, "Neuroscience and Dualism," 257, emphasis in original.
68. Egnor, "Neuroscience and Dualism," 258.
69. Cristi Cooper, "Free Will, Free Won't, and What the Libet Experiments Don't Tell Us," in Menuge et al., *Minding the Brain*, 171–272.
70. Andrea Lavazza and Mario De Caro, quoted in Cooper, "Free Will," 272.
71. Michael Egnor and Denyse O'Leary, *The Immortal Mind: A Neurosurgeon's Case for the Existence of the Soul* (New York: Worthy Publishing, 2025), 10.
72. Egnor and O'Leary, *The Immortal Mind*, 47–48, emphasis in original.
73. Egnor and O'Leary, *The Immortal Mind*, 48.
74. Egnor and O'Leary, *The Immortal Mind*, 58.
75. Gary R. Habermas, "Evidential Near-Death Experiences," in Menuge et al., *Minding the Brain*, 329.
76. Habermas, "Evidential Near-Death Experiences," 329.
77. Habermas, "Evidential Near-Death Experiences," 347.
78. Michael Ruse and E. O. Wilson, "The Evolution of Ethics," in James Huchingson, ed., *Religion and Natural Science: The Range of Engagement* (New York: Harcourt Brace Jovanovich, 1993), 210.
79. Allen Buchanan and Russell Powell. "The Limits of Evolutionary Explanations of Morality and Their Implications for Moral Progress," *Ethics* 126, no. 1 (2015): 38, https://doi.org/10.1086/682188.
80. "New Research Overturns Claim that Humans and Chimps Differ by Only 1% in Their DNA," *Discovery Institute*, May 21, 2025, https://www.discovery.org/a/new-research-overturns-claim-that-humans-and-chimps-differ-by-only-1-in-their-dna/.
81. DongAhn Yoo et al., "Complete Sequencing of Ape Genomes," *Nature* 641 (2025): 401–418, https://www.nature.com/articles/s41586-025-08816-3.
82. Webb, *The Arrogant Ape*, 154.
83. Unfortunately, fashionable or no, echoes of this poisonous racism persist today even among some who profess to be Christians. For more on the problem, see West, *Stockholm Syndrome Christianity*, 122; "'From One Man': Acts 17, Image Theology, and the Collapse of Mahler's Sanctification Hierarchy," *The Council*, May 19, 2025, https://watchmencouncil.com/2025/05/19/from-one-man-acts-17-image-theology-and-the-collapse-of-mahlers-sanctification-hierarchy/; and Phil Williams, "Meet the Hitler-Loving Podcast Who's Teaching Young Christian Men to Hate—in the Name Of God," *NewsChannel5 Nashville*, July 21, 2025, https://www.newschannel5.com/news/newschannel-5-investigates/confronting-hate/meet-the-hitler-loving-podcaster-whos-teaching-young-christian-men-to-hate-in-the-name-of-god.
84. "Fact Sheet: Human Genomic Variation," *National Human Genome Research Institute*, https://www.genome.gov/about-genomics/educational-resources/fact-sheets/human-genomic-variation.
85. Noah A. Rosenberg et al., "Genetic Structure of Human Populations," *Science* 298 (December 20, 2002): 2381.
86. Mateus H. Gouveia et al., "Subcontinental Genetic Variation in the *All of Us* Research Program: Implications for Biomedical Research," *The American Journal of Human Genetics* 112 (June 5, 2025): 1289.

87. Dylan J. Taylor et al., "Sources of Gene Expression Variation in a Globally Diverse Human Cohort," *Nature* 632 (July 17, 2024): 122, https://www.nature.com/articles/s41586-024-07708-2.

88. Lynn B. Jorde, "Genetic Variation and Human Evolution," October 16, 2003, https://www.ashg.org/wp-content/uploads/2019/09/genetic-variation-essay.pdf.

89. Adam Rutherford, "'Biological Reality': What Genetics Has Taught Us About Race," *BBC.com*, April 20, 2025, https://www.bbc.com/future/article/20250417-biological-reality-what-genetics-has-taught-us-about-race.

90. Jorde, "Genetic Variation and Human Evolution."

91. "ASHG Denounces Attempts to Link Genetics and Racial Supremacy," *The American Journal of Human Genetics* 103 (November 1, 2018): 636.

92. "ASHG Denounces Attempts to Link Genetics and Racial Supremacy."

93. National Academies of Sciences, Engineering, and Medicine, *Rethinking Race and Ethnicity in Biomedical Research* (Washington, DC: The National Academies Press, 2025), chap. 2, https://www.nationalacademies.org/read/27913/chapter/2.

94. Jonathan Kahn et al., "How Not to Talk About Race and Genetics," *BuzzFeed News*, March 30, 2018, https://www.buzzfeednews.com/article/bfopinion/race-genetics-david-reich. Also see Theresa N. Duello et al., "Race and Genetics Versus 'Race' in Genetics: A Systematic Review of the Use of African Ancestry in Genetic Studies," *Evolution, Medicine, and Public Health* 9, no. 1 (2021): 233, https://pmc.ncbi.nlm.nih.gov/articles/PMC8604262/.

95. Jennifer L. Baker, Charles N. Rotimi, and Daniel Shriner, "Human Ancestry Correlates with Language and Reveals That Race Is Not an Objective Genomic Classifier," *Scientific Reports* 7 (May 8, 2017): 1572, https://www.nature.com/articles/s41598-017-01837-7.

96. "How to Argue with a Racist: Five Myths Debunked," *BBC News*, March 16, 2020, https://www.bbc.co.uk/news/science-environment-51914782.amp.

97. Ajitha Reddy, "The Eugenics Origins of IQ Testing: Implications for Post-Atkins Litigation," *DePaul Law Review* 57, no. 3 (Spring 2008): 667, https://via.library.depaul.edu/law-review/vol57/iss3/5/; Aida Roige, "Intelligence and IQ Testing," *Eugenics Archive* (Canada), accessed December 17, 2025, https://www.eugenicsarchive.ca/encyclopedia?id=535eecb77095aa000000023a.

98. Ian J. Deary, Simon R. Cox, and W. David Hill, "Genetic Variation, Brain, and Intelligence Differences," *Molecular Psychiatry* 27 (2022): 347–348, https://www.nature.com/articles/s41380-021-01027-y.

99. David F. Marks, "IQ Variations Across Time, Race, and Nationality: An Artifact of Differences in Literacy Skills," *Psychological Reports* 106, no. 3 (2010): 643, https://doi.org/10.2466/pr0.106.3.643-664.

100. Callie H. Burt and Ronald L. Simons, "Pulling Back the Curtain on Heritability Studies: Biosocial Criminology in the Postgenomic Era," *Criminology* 52, no. 2 (2014): 251.

101. J. C. Barnes et al., "The Propensity for Aggressive Behavior and Lifetime Incarceration Risk: A Test for Gene-Environment Interaction (G X E) Using Whole-Genome Data," *Aggression and Violent Behavior* 49 (November-December 2019): 101307, https://doi.org/10.1016/j.avb.2019.07.002.

102. J. Wertz et al., "Genetics and Crime: Integrating New Genomic Discoveries into Psychological Research about Antisocial Behavior," *Psychological Science* 29, no. 5 (2018): 801.

103. Stefania Zampatti et al., "Genetic Variants Allegedly Linked to Antisocial Behavior Are Equally Distributed Across Different Population," *Journal of Personalized Medicine* 11, no. 3 (2021): 1, https://www.mdpi.com/2075-4426/11/3/213.
104. Zampatti, et al., "Genetic Variants," 6.
105. Zampatti, et al., "Genetic Variants," 7.
106. See West, *Stockholm Syndrome Christianity*, 144–145.
107. Jeffrey S. Adler, "Less Crime, More Punishment: Violence, Race, and Criminal Justice in Early Twentieth Century America," *The Journal of American History* 102, no. 1 (June 2015): 39–40.
108. Jefferson to Weightman, June 24, 1826.
109. "President Dwight D. Eisenhower's Farewell Address (1961)" (White House, Washington, DC, January 17, 1961), *National Archives*, https://www.archives.gov/milestone-documents/president-dwight-d-eisenhowers-farewell-address.
110. Nick Murray, "Time to Pull Back on Emergency Powers for Governors," *National Review*, February 16, 2021, https://www.nationalreview.com/2021/02/time-to-pull-back-on-emergency-powers-for-governors/.
111. "Governor Newsom to End the COVID-19 State of Emergency," *State of California: Governor Gavin Newsom*, October 17, 2022, https://www.gov.ca.gov/2022/10/17/governor-newsom-to-end-the-covid-19-state-of-emergency/.
112. Kevin Breuninger, "Fauci Blasts 'Preposterous' Covid Conspiracies, Accuses His Critics of 'Attacks on Science,'" *CNBC*, June 9, 2021, https://www.cnbc.com/2021/06/09/fauci-blasts-preposterous-covid-conspiracies-accuses-critics-of-attacks-on-science.html.
113. For examples, see *Free Science.Today* website, https://freescience.today/.
114. Hans A. von Spakovsky, "Prosecuting Climate Change 'Deniers' Is an Abuse of Power," *The Heritage Foundation*, April 22, 2016, https://www.heritage.org/environment/commentary/prosecuting-climate-change-deniers-abuse-power.
115. Hank Berrien, "Biden Calls for Social Media Censorship on Virus: 'Deal with the Misinformation and Disinformation," *The Daily Wire*, January 13, 2022, https://www.dailywire.com/news/biden-calls-for-social-media-censorship-on-virus-deal-with-the-misinformation-and-disinformation; "Confronting Health Misinformation: The US Surgeon General's Advisory on Building a Healthy Information Environment," *US Health and Human Services*, 2021, https://www.hhs.gov/sites/default/files/surgeon-general-misinformation-advisory.pdf.
116. Geoff Brumfiel, "This Doctor Spread False Information About COVID. She Still Kept Her Medical License," *NPR*, September 14, 2021, https://www.npr.org/sections/health-shots/2021/09/14/1035915598/doctors-covid-misinformation-medical-license.
117. US Senator Ron Johnson (@SenRonJohnson), "For the 5th Time this Year, @YouTube Is Censoring Me from Telling You the Truth," *Twitter*, November 12, 2021, 8:23 p.m., https://twitter.com/SenRonJohnson/status/1459346068131524609.
118. Quoted in Rachel Roubein, "NIH Director: 'Conspiracies Are Winning Here,'" *The Washington Post*, November 19, 2021, https://www.washingtonpost.com/politics/2021/11/19/nih-director-conspiracies-are-winning-here/.

119. Quoted in Berkeley Lovelace Jr., "Pfizer CEO Says People Who Spread Misinformation on Covid Vaccines Are 'Criminals,'" *CNBC*, November 9, 2021, https://www.cnbc.com/2021/11/09/covid-vaccines-pfizer-ceo-says-people-who-spread-misinformation-on-shots-are-criminals.html.
120. Brad Holyman, "As the Anniversary of the January 6 Insurrection Approaches, Senator Brad Hoylman Introduces Bill to Hold Tech Companies Accountable for Promoting Vaccine Misinformation & Hate Speech on Social Media," *New York State Senate*, December 27, 2021, https://www.nysenate.gov/newsroom/press-releases/brad-hoylman/anniversary-january-6-insurrection-approaches-senator-brad.
121. Senate Bill S7568, 2021–2022 Legislative Session, *New York State Senate*, https://www.nysenate.gov/legislation/bills/2021/s7568.
122. Jonathan Turley, "New York Considers Legislation to Curtail Free Speech in the Name of Democracy," *JonathanTurley.org*, December 30, 2021, https://jonathanturley.org/2021/12/30/new-york-considers-legislation-to-curtail-free-speech-in-the-name-of-democracy/.
123. AB 2098, California Assembly Bill, 2021-2022 Regular Session, https://openstates.org/ca/bills/20212022/AB2098/.
124. Ross Pomeroy, "How Is Sonia Sotomayor So Misinformed About COVID?," *Real Clear Science*, January 24, 2022, https://www.realclearscience.com/blog/2022/01/24/how_is_sonia_sotomayor_so_misinformed_about_covid_813303.html.
125. Harvey Risch, Robert W. Malone, and Byram Bridle, "Forcing People Into COVID Vaccines Ignores Important Scientific Information," *The Federalist*, December 14, 2021, https://thefederalist.com/2021/12/14/forcing-people-into-covid-vaccines-ignores-important-scientific-information/.
126. OpenVAERS, accessed January 8, 2026, https://openvaers.com/.
127. John Milton, *Areopagitica* [1644], https://milton.host.dartmouth.edu/reading_room/areopagitica/text.shtml.
128. Otto Bounds, "Letter: Stop Mincing Words: They're Parasites, Not Patriots," *Yakima Herald*, August 18, 2021, https://www.yakimaherald.com/opinion/letter-stop-mincing-words-theyre-parasites-not-patriots/article_7513f68b-20ab-5a6c-8543-f937767e2acd.html.
129. Betty Seidmon-Vidibor, letter to the editor, *The Los Angeles Times*, January 1, 2022, https://www.latimes.com/opinion/letters-to-the-editor/story/2022-01-01/readers-end-2021-angry-over-covid.
130. Rachel Charlton-Dailey, "Op-Ed: Unvaccinated People Are Not Oppressed—They're Dangerous," *Very Well Health*, November 30, 2021, https://web.archive.org/web/20220202013538/https://www.verywellhealth.com/unvaccinated-people-are-not-oppressed-5210475.
131. Victoria Paterno, MD, letter to the editor, *The Los Angeles Times*, July 21, 2021, https://web.archive.org/web/20220202013556/https://www.msn.com/en-us/news/us/letters-to-the-editor-i-ve-had-enough-readers-are-furious-at-vaccine-refusers/ar-AAMoqNx.
132. Stephen Dinan, "Federal Judge Blasts Unvaccinated Jurors as 'Selfish and Unpatriotic,'" *The Washington Times*, January 20, 2022, https://www.washingtontimes.com/news/2022/jan/20/robert-n-scola-jr-federal-judge-blasts-unvaccinate/.

133. Cillian Breathnach, "Gene Simmons Says 'Delusional, Evil' Unvaccinated People Are the 'Enemy,' Compares Them to Flat-Earthers," *Guitar.com*, November 12, 2021, https://guitar.com/news/music-news/gene-simmons-antivax-antii-vaccine-flat-earth-enemy/.

134. Nelson Oliveira, "This State Has Both the Country's Lowest Vaccination Rate and IQ Score. See How Other States Measure Up," *New York Daily News*, May 24, 2021, https://www.nydailynews.com/news/national/ny-states-lowest-highest-vaccination-rates-iq-score-covid-20210524-ubkwdphohrabbi77vurazmwehe-story.html.

135. "Alabama Governor: It's Time to Start Blaming Unvaccinated Folks," *CNN*, July 23, 2021, https://www.cnn.com/videos/us/2021/07/23/alabama-governor-ivey-covid-19-vaccinations-newsroom-vpx.cnn.

136. David Frum (@DavidFrum), "But the Malignant Minority… ," *Twitter*, December 12, 2021, 7:59 a.m., https://twitter.com/davidfrum/status/1470030543953838088.

137. Kendra Cherry, "What Is Othering?," *Very Well Mind*, December 13, 2020, https://www.verywellmind.com/what-is-othering-5084425.

138. West, *Darwin Day in America*, 139–140.

139. John West, "Francis Collins' Rhetoric About the Unvaccinated Is Anything but Christian," *The Stream*, September 29, 2021, https://stream.org/francis-collins-rhetoric-about-the-unvaccinated-is-anything-but-christian/.

140. David French, "It's Time to Stop Rationalizing and Enabling Evangelical Vaccine Rejection," *The Dispatch*, August 29, 2021, https://thedispatch.com/newsletter/frenchpress/its-time-to-stop-rationalizing-christian/.

141. Natalie Sherman, "Vaccine Mandates: 'I Lost My Job for Being Unvaccinated,'" *BBC News*, January 23, 2022, https://web.archive.org/web/20220124010839/https://news.yahoo.com/vaccine-mandates-lost-job-being-004347955.html.

142. Josephine Nesbit, "Workers Fired for Being Unvaccinated May Not Be Able to Collect Unemployment Benefits," *MSN Finance*, August 9, 2021, https://web.archive.org/web/20220131160956/https://www.msn.com/en-us/money/personalfinance/workers-fired-for-being-unvaccinated-may-not-be-able-to-collect-unemployment-benefits/ar-AAN74ld.

143. Marquise Francis, "Medical Ethicists Criticize Doctors Refusing to Treat the Unvaccinated," *Yahoo!* News, September 24, 2021, https://news.yahoo.com/medical-ethicists-criticize-doctors-refusing-to-treat-the-unvaccinated-202958236.html.

144. Christina Coulter, "Boston Hospital REMOVES Dying Father-Of-Two, 31, from Top of Heart Transplant List Because He's Not Vaccinated: His Father Says 'My Son Has Gone to the Edge of Death to Stick to His Guns,'" *Dailymail.com*, January 25, 2022, https://www.dailymail.co.uk/news/article-10439735/Boston-father-two-31-removed-heart-transplant-list-hes-not-vaccinated.html?ito=social-twitter_mailonline.

145. "Proof of Vaccination," *Town of Oakville*, Canada, February 2, 2022, https://web.archive.org/web/20220202013542/https://www.oakville.ca/townhall/proof-of-vaccination.html.

146. Alan Evans, "Judge Denies Mom Custody of Son Because She's Unvaccinated," *The Daily Signal*, August 30, 2021, https://www.dailysignal.com/2021/08/30/judge-denies-mom-custody-of-son-because-shes-unvaccinated/.

147. "Utah Leaders Have Surrendered to COVID Pandemic, the Editorial Board Writes," *The Salt Lake City Tribune*, January 14, 2022, https://www.sltrib.com/opinion/editorial/2022/01/15/utah-leaders-have/.

148. "COVID-19: Democratic Voters Support Harsh Measures Against Unvaccinated," *Rasmussen Reports*, January 13, 2022, https://www.rasmussenreports.com/public_content/politics/partner_surveys/jan_2022/covid_19_democratic_voters_support_harsh_measures_against_unvaccinated.

149. "COVID-19 Cases and Hospitalizations by COVID-19 Vaccination Status and Previous COVID-19 Diagnosis—California and New York, May–November 2021," *Centers for Disease Control and Prevention*, January 28, 2021, https://www.cdc.gov/mmwr/volumes/71/wr/mm7104e1.htm?s_cid=mm7104e1_w.

150. Smitha Mundasad, "Covid: Children's Extremely Low Risk Confirmed by Study," *BBC*, July 9, 2021, https://www.bbc.com/news/health-57766717.

151. "State Surgeon General Dr. Joseph A. Ladapo Issues New mRNA COVID-19 Vaccine Guidance," *Florida Department of Health*, October 7, 2021, https://content.govdelivery.com/accounts/FLDOH/bulletins/3312697. Also see Supriya S. Jain et al., "Cardiac Manifestations and Outcomes of COVID-19 Vaccine-Associated Myocarditis in the Young in the USA: Longitudinal Results from the Myocarditis After COVID Vaccination (MACiv) Multicenter Study," *eClinical Medicine* 76 (October 2024): 102809, https://www.thelancet.com/journals/eclinm/article/PIIS2589-5370(24)00388-2/fulltext; and Alexander Tin, "FDA Expands COVID Vaccine Warning About Heart Side Effect Risk for Young Males," *CBS News*, May 21, 2025, https://www.cbsnews.com/news/fda-covid-vaccine-mrna-heart-side-effects-warning-label/.

152. "After Action Review of the Covid-19 Pandemic: The Lessons Learned and a Path Forward, Final Report of the Select Subcommittee on the Coronavirus Pandemic," *Committee on Oversight and Accountability, US House of Representatives*, December 4, 2024, https://oversight.house.gov/wp-content/uploads/2024/12/2024.12.04-SSCP-FINAL-REPORT-ANS.pdf.

153. "After Action Review," 292.

154. "After Action Review," 198.

155. "After Action Review,"207.

156. "After Action Review," 214.

157. "After Action Review," 346.

158. "After Action Review," 340.

159. Jonas Herby, Lars Jonung, and Steve H. Hanke, "Were COVID-190 Lockdowns Worth It? A Meta-Analysis," *Public Choice* 203 (2024): 355, https://doi.org/10.1007/s11127-024-01216-7.

160. Alex R. Piquero et al., "Domestic Violence During the COVID-19 Pandemic—Evidence from a Systematic Review and Meta-Analysis," *Journal of Criminal Justice* 74 (2021): 101806, https://doi.org/10.1016/j.jcrimjus.2021.101806.

161. Ambarish Chandra and Tracy Beth Høeg, "Lack of Correlation Between School Mask Mandates and Paediatric COVID-19 Cases in a Large Cohort," *Journal of Infection* 85, no. 6 (2022): P671–675, https://doi.org/10.1016/j.jinf.2022.09.019.

162. See the helpful review of issues in David Gortler and Jay Richards, "Why Did President Trump Get an mRNA COVID-19 Shot?" *The Daily Signal*, October 27,

2025, https://www.dailysignal.com/2025/10/27/why-did-president-trump-get-an-mrna-covid-19-shot/; K. Faksova et al., "COVID-19 Vaccines and Adverse Events of Special Interest: A Multinational Global Vaccine Data Network (GVDN) Cohort Study of 99 Million Vaccinated Individuals," *Vaccine* 42, no. 9 (2024): 2200–2211, https://www.sciencedirect.com/science/article/pii/S0264410X24001270?via%3Dihub.

163. "Changes to State Emergency Power Laws in Response to the Coronavirus (COVE-19) Pandemic, 2020–2023," *Ballotpedia*, https://ballotpedia.org/Changes_to_state_emergency_power_laws_in_response_to_the_coronavirus_(COVID-19)_pandemic,_2020–2023.

164. Richard R. Hammar and Matthew Branaugh, "Assessing US Supreme Court Rulings on Pandemic Restrictions," *ChurchLaw&Tax*, April 23, 2021, https://www.churchlawandtax.com/stay-legal/church-state/assessing-us-supreme-court-rulings-on-pandemic-restrictions/.

165. "John MacArthur and Grace Community Church Win $800,000 Settlement from California and L.A. County," *Standing for Freedom Center*, September 1, 2021, https://www.standingforfreedom.com/2021/09/01/john-macarthur-and-grace-community-church-win-800000-settlement-from-california-and-l-a-county/.

166. Mark Zuckerberg, CEO, Meta Platforms, Inc. to Jim Jordan, Chairman, Committee on the Judiciary, United States House of Representatives. The text of the letter does not appear to be available on an official government site, but a scan was posted by House Judiciary GOP (@JudiciaryGOP), *Twitter*, August 26, 2024, 5:44 p.m., https://x.com/JudiciaryGOP/status/1828201780544504064/photo/1.

167. Letter from Daniel F. Donovan, Counsel for Alphabet to Jim Jordan, Chairman, Committee on the Judiciary, United States House of Representatives, September 23, 2025, https://judiciary.house.gov/sites/evo-subsites/republicans-judiciary.house.gov/files/evo-media-document/2025-09-23-letter-to-hjc.pdf.

168. "Jay Bhattacharya Begins Tenure as 18th Director of the National Institutes of Health," *National Institutes of Health*, April 1, 2025, https://www.nih.gov/news-events/news-releases/jay-bhattacharya-begins-tenure-18th-director-national-institutes-health.

169. "Great Barrington Declaration," *Great Barrington Declaration*, accessed January 8, 2026, https://gbdeclaration.org/.

170. "Jay Bhattacharya Curriculum Vitae," *Stanford*, https://web.stanford.edu/~jay/CV-Jay-June2021.pdf.

171. Vinay Prasad, "At a Time When the U.S. Needed Covid-19 Dialogue Between Scientists, Francis Collins Moved to Shut It Down," *STAT*, December 23, 2021, https://www.statnews.com/2021/12/23/at-a-time-when-the-u-s-needed-covid-19-dialogue-between-scientists-francis-collins-moved-to-shut-it-down/.

172. Richard Payerchin, "Bhattacharya Outlines Plan to Restore Credibility at National Institutes of Health," *Medical Economics*, March 5, 2025, https://www.medicaleconomics.com/view/bhattacharya-outlines-plan-to-restore-credibility-at-national-institutes-of-health; Jay Bhattacharya, "Dr. Jay Goes to Washington: Reforming Science from the Inside at NIH," interview by Peter Robinson, *Uncommon Knowledge*, May 28, 2025, https://www.hoover.org/research/dr-jay-goes-washington-reforming-science-inside-nih; Tim Haines, "NIH Director

Dr. Jay Bhattacharya: Honesty and Transparency Will Get Better Results Than Vaccine Mandates," *RealClearPolitics*, September 5, 2025, https://www.realclearpolitics.com/video/2025/09/05/nih_director_dr_jay_bhattacharya_.html.

173. John G. West, "Frightening Recommendations from Francis Collins," December 5, 2024, *Science & Culture Today*, https://scienceandculture.com/2024/12/frightening-recommendations-from-francis-collins/.

174. John G. West, *How Americans View the American Founding* (Discovery Institute, 2026), 13, https://endowedbyourcreator.com/survey.

175. "What Is WPATH and What Are Their Guidelines?" *Clinical Advisory Network on Sex and Gender*, 2025, https://can-sg.org/frequently-asked-questions/what-is-wpath-and-what-are-their-guidelines/; "WPATH Influence Undermines WHO's Transgender Guidelines," *Society for Evidence Based Gender Medicine*, July 11, 2024, https://segm.org/wpath-evidence-manipulation-risks-discrediting-WHO-transgender-guidelines; "Scandalous Suppression of Research on Transgender Health," *Clinical Advisory Network on Sex and Gender*, 2025, https://can-sg.org/2024/06/28/scandalous-suppression-of-research-on-transgender-health/.

176. G. Samantha Rosenthal, "Pseudoscience Has Long Been Used to Oppress Transgender People," *Scientific American*, February 12, 2024, https://www.scientificamerican.com/article/pseudoscience-has-long-been-used-to-oppress-transgender-people/.

177. Justice Clarence Thomas, Concurring Opinion, *United States v. Skrmetti*, 605 US (2025), 7, https://www.supremecourt.gov/opinions/24pdf/23-477_2cp3.pdf.

178. *Buck v. Bell*, 274 U.S. 200 (1927), https://supreme.justia.com/cases/federal/us/274/200/.

179. Thomas, Concurring Opinion, *United States v. Skrmetti*, 22–23.

CHAPTER 6: WHERE DO WE GO FROM HERE?

1. Paul Simon, *Freedom's Champion: Elijah Lovejoy* (Carbondale, IL: Southern Illinois UP,1994), 45–48. For details about mob violence in American history, see Stefan Lund, "The Dangerous Misunderstanding of America's History of Mob Action," *History News Network*, July 21, 2022, https://www.historynewsnetwork.org/article/the-dangerous-misunderstanding-of-americas-history.

2. "Timeline About the Life and Career of Abraham Lincoln," *Lincoln Memorial Shrine*, accessed December 17, 2025, https://www.lincolnshrine.org/wp-content/uploads/2020/03/Timeline-of-Lincolns-Life.pdf.

3. Abraham Lincoln, "Lyceum Address" (Young Men's Lyceum, Springfield, IL, January 27, 1838), *Abraham Lincoln Online*, https://www.abrahamlincolnonline.org/lincoln/speeches/lyceum.htm.

4. Quoted in John G. West, *Walt Disney and Live Action: The Disney Studio's Live-Action Features of the 1950s and 60s* (United States: Theme Park Press, 2016), 84–85.

5. "Tuesday, August 17, 1858," *The Lincoln Log: A Daily Chronology of the Life of Abraham Lincoln*, accessed December 17, 2025, https://www.thelincolnlog.org/Results.aspx?type=CalendarDay&day=1858-08-17; William Proctor to Abraham Lincoln, August 6, 1858, note 5, *Abraham Lincoln Presidential Library and Museum: Papers of Abraham Lincoln Digital Library*, https://papersofabrahamlincoln.org/documents/D210845.

6. Abraham Lincoln, "Speech at Lewiston, Illinois," August 17, 1858, account published by *Chicago Press and Tribune*, August 21, 1858, *University of Michigan Library Digital Collections: Collected Works of Abraham Lincoln*, https://quod.lib.umich.edu/cgi/t/text/text-idx?c=lincoln;cc=lincoln;view=text;idno=lincoln2;rgn=div1;node=lincoln2:567#2_544_1.
7. Lincoln, "Speech at Lewiston, Illinois," emphasis in original. Paragraph breaks added.

Acknowledgments

Like many Americans, I am a product of the melting pot. On my father's side, my ancestors reach back to New England in the 1600s. One of them helped found Hartford, Connecticut. A great-great grandfather fought for the Union in the Battle of Gettysburg. On my mother's side, both of my grandparents came to America before World War I from what is now Ukraine, and my mother grew up in Connecticut and New York as the daughter of Ukrainian immigrants. New or old, both strands of my family loved America and were grateful for its blessings. This book could not have been written without the love of America faithfully passed down to me from my parents and their forebears.

The present book also couldn't have been written without the wisdom of those who taught me in graduate school, where I had the good providence to study the American Founding with Harry Jaffa, Charles Kesler, William Allen, and Leonard Levy, each a giant in his own right. I remain indebted to all of them. After graduate school, I was hired by Discovery Institute founder Bruce Chapman, from whom I learned many more things about America. With a distinguished career spanning both elective and appointive office, Bruce is an exemplar of the thoughtful and civic-minded citizen in public life who isn't supposed to exist anymore in America. Bruce also loves to think outside the box, which led to the founding of Discovery Institute's Center for Science and Culture by Stephen Meyer and myself, as described in Chapter 5, a chapter that owes much to the work of my colleagues at the Center.

I am grateful for those who read, commented on, and improved the manuscript with their suggestions, including Lucas Morel, William Allen, Ken Masugi, Mark David Hall, Brian Miller, and my wife, Sonja. The book was further enriched by meticulous editing, polishing, and proofing from Jonathan and Amanda Witt; professional layout by Sandra Jurca; and an arresting cover by Nathan Jacobson. I am thankful to those who took time from their busy schedules to write endorsements, and I am grateful for being encouraged in this project by Discovery Institute's president Steven Buri. Finally, I would like to express my gratitude to Dr. Gerson Moreno-Riaño, president of Cornerstone University. I met Dr. Moreno-Riaño during the latter part of writing this book when he invited me to speak at Cornerstone about my last book. His passion for the future of America is contagious, and because of him, many students may be exposed to the ideas in this book in years to come.

Image Credits

Facing Title Page
Engraving of original Declaration of Independence. Public domain.

Figure 1.1. The original Declaration of Independence on display at the Jefferson Memorial in 1943. Library of Congress, Prints & Photographs Division, FSA/OWI Collection, https://www.loc.gov/pictures/item/2017697616/. Public domain.

Figure 1.2. The "Dunlap Broadside," the first printed version of the Declaration of Independence, July 1776, printed by John Dunlap of Philadelphia. Public domain.

Figure 1.3. First reading of the Declaration of Independence in Philadelphia by John Nixon. Image published in *Harper's Weekly,* July 15, 1876. Public domain. | Reading of the Declaration of Independence from the east balcony of the Old State House, Boston, MA, July 18, 1776. George Washington Bicentennial Commission, 1931–32. National Archives, https://catalog.archives.gov/id/532942. Public domain. | First reading of the Declaration of Independence in New York. Image published in *Harper's Weekly,* 1870. Library of Congress, https://www.loc.gov/pictures/item/89706308/. Public domain.

Figure 1.4. *Top:* Asher Durand's engraving (1823) of John Trumbull's iconic painting "The Declaration of Independence." Wikimedia Commons. Public domain. *Second row, left:* One of the earliest known decorative reproductions of the original Declaration of Independence, produced by Benjamin Owen Tyler, 1818. National Archives, https://catalog.archives.gov/id/505689254. Public domain. *Second row, right:* Copperplate engraving of the original Declaration of Independence, commissioned by John Quincy Adams and completed in 1823, https://catalog.archives.gov/id/1656605. Public domain.

Figure 1.5. *Top*: Reading of the Declaration of Independence at Independence Hall in Philadelphia on July 4, 1876, by Richard Henry Lee, grandson of signer of the Declaration of same name. Public domain. *Bottom*: Chamber in Independence Hall where the Declaration was adopted by the Continental Congress, as it appeared in 1876. The original Declaration was put on display in this room in a special safe from early 1876 to early 1877. Public domain.

Figure 1.6. Librarian of Congress Herbert Putnam installing the Declaration of Independence in its new display case at the Library of Congress, February 1924. Library of Congress, https://www.loc.gov/pictures/item/2016848736/. Public domain.

Figure 1.7. President and Mrs. Coolidge at the dedication of the public display of the Declaration of Independence and the Constitution in the Great Hall of the Library of Congress. Library of Congress, https://www.loc.gov/pictures/item/2016846647/. Public domain.

Figure 1.8. *Top:* Publicity photo for *Mr. Smith Goes to Washington*. Moviestore Collection Ltd./Alamy. *Bottom:* Publicity poster for *Mr. Smith Goes to Washington*. Columbia Pictures, 1939. Public domain.

Figure 1.9. World War II poster featuring the Declaration of Independence. Office of War Information, 1942–1945. National Archives, https://catalog.archives.gov/id/7387467. Public domain.

Figure 1.10. *Top:* Freedom Train promotional material, 1949. National Archives, https://catalog.archives.gov/id/12167255. *Bottom:* Visitors to the Freedom Train viewing Thomas Jefferson's draft of the Declaration of Independence, 1948. National Archives, https://catalog.archives.gov/id/12167320. Public domain.

Figure 1.11. *Top:* Transfer of the "Charters of Freedom" (including the Declaration of Independence) from the Library of Congress to the National Archives, December 1952. National Archives, https://catalog.archives.gov/id/12167992. Public domain. *Bottom:* Installation of the Declaration of Independence in new exhibit case in the National Archives, December 1952. National Archives, https://catalog.archives.gov/id/7657226. Public domain.

Figure 1.12. *Top:* President Truman participates in the unveiling of the new Charters of Freedom exhibit at the National Archives, featuring the Declaration, the Constitution, and the Bill of Rights, December 1952. Photographer: Abbie Rowe, National Park Service. National Archives, https://catalog.archives.gov/id/338959186. Public domain. *Bottom:* Congressman Gerald Ford shows constituents the Declaration of Independence at the National Archives in July 1955. National Archives, https://catalog.archives.gov/id/6923712. Public domain.

Figure 1.13. Replica of Independence Hall at Knott's Berry Farm, Buena Park, CA. ©John G. West, 2017.

Figure 1.14. *Top:* Publicity photo from *National Treasure* (2004). BFA/Touchstone Pictures/Alamy. ©Columbia Pictures. *Bottom:* Poster for *National Treasure* (2004). Moviestore Collection Ltd./Alamy. ©Columbia Pictures.

Figure 2.1. Draft of the Declaration of Independence in the hand of Thomas Jefferson. Wikimedia Commons. Public domain.

Figure 2.2. *Each row, left to right, starting at the top:* Thomas Jefferson, Benjamin Franklin, John Adams, James Wilson, John Witherspoon, Benjamin Rush. Wikimedia Commons. Public domain.

Figure 2.3. *Each row, left to right, starting at the top:* Isaac Newton, John Ray, Bishop Joseph Butler, Archbishop François Fénelon, Samuel Clarke, Francis Hutcheson. Wikimedia Commons. Public domain.

Figure 3.1. Alexander H. Stephens (1812–1883), Vice President of the Confederacy. Wikimedia Commons. Public domain.

Figure 3.2. Comparison of the cranial anatomy of a European (Greek), a black man, and a chimpanzee in J. C. Nott and Geo. R. Gliddon, *Types of Mankind* (1854), 458. Public domain.

Figure 4.1. Ota Benga (c. 1883–1916), an African man from the Congo, put on public display in the primate house at the Bronx Zoo in 1906. Bain News Service. Library of Congress, Prints & Photographs Division, https://www.loc.gov/pictures/item/2014702691/. Public domain.

Figure 4.2. *Each row, left to right, starting at the top:* Charles Darwin, William McGee, Charles Davenport, Edward East, Charles Francis Adams Jr., Benjamin Tillman. Wikimedia Commons. Public domain.

Figure 4.3. Proponents of the new "scientific" theory of politics. *Each row, left to right, starting at the top:* John Burgess, Charles Merriam, Westel Willoughby, Woodrow Wilson, Carl Becker. Wikimedia Commons. Public domain.

Figure 4.4. Eugenics exhibition at the American Museum of Natural History in 1932. From *A Decade of Progress in Eugenics: Scientific Papers of the Third International Congress of Eugenics* (Baltimore: The Williams & Wilkins Company, 1934), plate 1. This book is believed to be in the public domain.

Figure 5.1. "Woodland Landscape" (1850) by Asher Brown Durand. Wikimedia Commons. Public domain.

Figure 5.2. Noted scientists who have thought there is evidence of design or purpose in nature. *Each row, left to right, starting at the top:* Fred Hoyle, American Institute of Physics (AIP), Attribution via Wikimedia Commons. | Charles Townes, Wikimedia commons. Public domain. | Freeman Dyson (1923–2020), ioerror, CC BY-SA 2.0 via Wikimedia Commons. | Nobel laureate physicist Brian Josephson, Cavendish Laboratory, CC BY-SA 3.0 via Wikimedia Commons.

Figure 5.3. Comparison of animal vs. human technology. *Each row, left to right, starting at the top:* Chimpanzee with branch, © Clivia/Adobe Stock. Beaver's dam, ©nyker/Adobe Stock. Bulldozer, ©Kadmy/Adobe Stock. Notre Dame Cathedral, ©TTstudio/Adobe Stock. Person working at a computer, ©DC Studio/Adobe Stock. Jet airplane, ©Frank Peters/Adobe Stock.

Figure 5.4. *Top:* President Dwight Eisenhower. Wikimedia Commons. Public domain. *Bottom:* Page from Eisenhower's Farewell Address, where he warned about the rise of "a scientific-technological elite." National Archives, https://www.archives.gov/milestone-documents/president-dwight-d-eisenhowers-farewell-address. Public domain.

Figure 6.1. Statue of Abraham Lincoln (1809–1865) in the Lincoln Memorial, Washington, DC. ©Wendy Kaveney/Adobe Stock.

Index

I

J

K

L

M

R

S

T

www.ingramcontent.com/pod-product-compliance
Lightning Source LLC
LaVergne TN
LVHW091143080826
845145LV00008B/2235

9781637120873